MULTINATIONAL ENTERPRISES AND
GOVERNMENT INTERVENTION

MULTINATIONAL ENTERPRISES & GOVERNMENT INTERVENTION

Thomas A. Poynter

ST. MARTIN'S PRESS
New York

© 1985 Thomas A. Poynter
All rights reserved. For information, write:
St. Martin's Press, Inc., 175 Fifth Avenue,
New York, NY 10010
First Published in the United States of America in 1985

Library of Congress Cataloging in Publication Data

Poynter, Thomas A.
    Multinational enterprises and government
    intervention.
    Includes index.
    1. Industry and state.
    2. International business enterprises.
    I. Title.
    HD3611.P67 1985   338.8'8   85–2078
    ISBN 0–312–55256–4

Typeset by Mayhew Typesetting, Bristol, UK
Printed and bound in Great Britain

CONTENTS

115221

LIST OF TABLES AND FIGURES

Tables

Figures

TO

DONALD A. POYNTER

AND

FLORENCE M. POYNTER

1 INTRODUCTION

Government regulation and intervention has always been an important factor in international business operations. The impact of government's role varies from country to country, and in the same country, from industry to industry and even from firm to firm. While some forms of government intervention such as financial support and trade protection are often sought by international firms, most government intervention is costly to them.

Corporate reaction to government intervention which adversely affects operations has varied. Some firms aggressively attempt to control such behaviour directly, while others treat intervention as a fact of life over which they have little, if any, control. Politically-able firms attempt to change either the legislation, or at least its implementation.

The form of *intervention* has been changing since the mid-1960s. It is clear that many nations have been eschewing such extreme actions as expropriation in favour of other, less extreme, methods designed to change the behaviour of firms and increase the domestic share of the investment's benefits. Extreme actions, nations found, affect financial ratings, deter other foreign investors and are not necessary to achieve their goals. Increasingly, intervention activities seem to be directed toward such goals as the partial transfer of ownership and control, greater domestic value-added and employing and promoting more host nationals. These less extreme activities are far more frequent and have a far greater impact on foreign investors than their high profile precedents.

Examinations of these more frequently occurring interventions has allowed the phenomenon to be better understood. The findings suggest that intervention is to a large extent explainable and predictable. International firms, it seems, are not really powerless to affect the impact of intervention or its frequency. Firms can introduce strategies to reduce undesired intervention and, in addition, provide themselves with an accurate assessment of the risks involved. Intervention can, in other words, be managed.

The purpose of this book is to report what has been learned over the past decade or so about the management of intervention. It does this by first looking for patterns in the intervention behaviour of governments around the world. My research and experiences and those of

1

other academics and consultants are used as the basis for identifying existing patterns of intervention behaviour. The book then focuses on a corporate survival plan that describes how firms can monitor their exposure to intervention and seek to reduce it.

While the lessons reported in this book apply to most kinds of international direct investors, generally it is directed at the larger, multi-country investors referred to as multinational enterprises (MNEs). This book will evaluate ways MNEs can seek to reduce their vulnerability to intervention directed at foreign-owned operations. While such intervention occurs in almost all countries, this report is concerned primarily with those countries where it is more common: the less-developed countries (LDCs) and the newly-industrialized countries (NICs). The fundamentals learned, however, apply equally to developed nations with an interventionist record in the operations of foreign-owned firms.

The Intervention Problem

The West German subsidiary in Brazil whose operations have been 'reserved' for Brazilian firms, the UK subsidiary in Nigeria which is ordered to 'sell' 60 per cent of its shareholding to Nigerian interests and the US subsidiary in India which is not allowed to expand or import needed components are all experiencing intervention. These interventions cause foreign-owned firms to lose assets, subject the subsidiary to external influence and a forced sharing of earnings, and place the firm at a competitive disadvantage compared to other, less affected, foreign and domestic competitors.

The scope of modern intervention is wide. In addition to the above examples, foreign-owned firms face requirements to export into a highly competitive free market while being forced to source components from a high cost host market, as well as government pressure to accept payments in the form of goods and commodities. *Expropriations* and *nationalizations*, while infrequent today, had the advantage of at least being insurable risks. Present day interventions reduce overseas profits, take up senior management time, distort trading and intra-firm sourcing patterns and, with a few exceptions, are not covered by political risk insurance.

The result is that many MNEs are finding investment in all but a handful of countries provides highly uncertain earnings. This prompts disinvestment and the milking of subsidiary operations overseas. While the vocal criticism levelled at MNEs during the 1970s has declined, MNEs are hesitant to publically criticize host government interventionist behaviour, and their traditional approach to managing intervention is increasingly ineffective. The choice facing MNEs is to reformulate their approach to government intervention, or, to continue de-emphasizing foreign direct investment.

The Traditional Management of Intervention

The *traditional* manner in which multinational enterprises manage government intervention can more accurately be described as their 'response to' rather than the 'management of' intervention [Behrman, Boddewyn and Kapoor, 1975, p. 45 *et seq.*]. Firms generally attempt to modify either the intervention policy, or its effects on the firm, *after* the decision to intervene has been made. Their traditional responses can be classified into three types:

1. the negotiation or forcing of changes in the intervention policy;
2. attempts to avoid or bypass the policy; and
3. taking intervention as a given and then avoiding nations where intervention is, or is expected to be, high.

Negotiating or forcing change in a conceived or proclaimed intervention policy is an uphill struggle under most circumstances. Civil servants and politicians find it difficult to recant in the face of all but the strongest of threats. Government departments, companies, shareholders and employees likely to gain from the proposed intervention will also act to counter any MNE pressures. In short, considerable MNE resources and time is necessary to modify an intervention policy after it has been promulgated. An easier way to redirect the impact of intervention is to modify the implementation of the policy so as to reduce its costs to the firm. Pressing the host interventionists to interpret the policy less strictly, perhaps in return for concessions less costly to the firm, seems to meet with greater success than attempts to change the original policy.

The success of those corporate responses is dependent on what concessions or counter-proposals the foreign firm can offer to the proponents of intervention. The foreign firm's *home government* may also offer some support by acting on the firm's behalf. In an

increasingly interdependent world the scope for governments to inter-
act covers quite a wide spectrum, ranging from aid to political support
in multinational agencies and forums.

There are fundamental disadvantages to these traditional responses
to intervention. First, the firm is on the defensive, which often requires
it to be somewhat excessive as it defends itself. Secondly, the firm is
trying to change the intervention from the planned high level to a lower
level. In other words, the explicit starting point for any negotiations
is a high and costly level of intervention. While negotiations and trade-
offs may reduce intervention somewhat, the interventionists' aspirations
and political complications generally ensure a less than satisfactory
outcome for the foreign firm.

The second corporate response to intervention can be regarded as
an attempt at avoiding or bypassing intervention. Firms attempt to find
loopholes in legislation only to discover that many governments are not
at all hampered by poorly drafted laws. Governments seldom discriminate between corporate avoidance and evasion. Blatant refusal to co-
operate often results in retaliation by intervention sponsors.

The only kinds of firms which appear to succeed with the avoidance
alternative are small low-profile firms, which attract little public attention. They escape intervention during its enforcement stage primarily
due to the existence of overworked civil servants and the fact that the
firms' small size makes them relatively undesirable to interventionists,
considering the amount of effort required. For most firms, however,
the avoidance option at best just delays the intervention.

The final type of response to intervention is prevalent in almost all
firms: to evade nations where intervention is, or is expected to be, high.
This procedure fails on two counts. First, the history of private foreign
direct investment is littered with examples of 'safe' host nations which
turned out to have a high level of intervention, for example Brazil, Iran,
Mexico and Canada. Although they do not achieve the same degree of
attention, there are even more examples of countries which intervene
much less than expected, for example 1970s Indonesia, Ivory Coast and
Pakistan. In spite of the myriad of political risk indices and research
by political scientists and presumably interested intelligence agencies,
forecasts of national rates of intervention seem to be unreliable.

The second reason why this country-avoidance strategy fails is that
it erroneously assumes that *all* firms experience high intervention in
a country with a high average level of intervention. In fact there is
a considerable amount of variation among firms. It is therefore, incorrect for an individual firm to assume that it will automatically suffer

because the average national level of intervention is high. For instance, a major blow to the automobile companies in Mexico several years ago was the government's strict limit on vertical integration. Instead of Ford, GM, Nissan and others being allowed to use their own body stamping operations, the Mexican government forced them to purchase from Mexican-owned suppliers. Volkswagen, however, was successful in obtaining an exemption and procured a competitive advantage from their own, lower cost, stamping plant.

Equally, firms have unfortunately discovered that safety is not assured in nations with *low* average intervention. Many of the simpler consumer goods firms in Indonesia or low-technology manufacturers in Singapore have found that governments do indeed discriminate among firms when they intervene.

Overall, then, multinational firms have traditionally handled intervention in extreme and rather ineffective ways. In many situations, their approach has been one of reaction rather than a more pro-active, or at least a prepared, management of intervention.

The disadvantages of these strategies are expressed in their lack of success in reducing the cost and level of intervention; in the poor public and private images of multinationals as they try to evade 'legitimate' government decrees; and in the foreclosing of potentially attractive investment opportunities when firms react by reducing or avoiding investment. The purpose of this book is to discuss and evaluate alternative methods for intervention management.

Objectives

The search for lessons to be learned from the interplay between the sovereign state and the multinational enterprise is recent. The major work of Raymond Vernon just over a decade ago involved an historical examination of the problems and prospects of multinationals since the middle of the nineteenth century. His examination of what he called, '. . . the waxing and waning of the power' of the MNE concluded that such power was a function of company and industry characteristics (1971, p. 26).

Raymond Vernon's work on what has come to be called intervention dealt primarily with the natural resource sector. In addition, the concept of managing one's intervention risk, rather than having it pre-ordained by industrial and technological changes, received little attention. This book will examine manufacturing interests in detail, and focus on the management issues.

The overall objective of this book is to provide managers in multi-national enterprises with sufficient information so that they can better devise feasible global strategies which allow them to manage intervention. In this sense, the management of intervention is similar to the management of financial or marketing problems. Successful management allows the firm better to predict changes in intervention, allows better assessment of risk and, given one's ability to affect the level of intervention, it allows the firm to reduce the level and cost of intervention it experiences.

The greatest drawback to successful management appears to be the complexity of implementing global management systems. This book's objective is to report on successful and unsuccessful attempts by multinationals to manage intervention, and it draws from this examination some general strategies.

The successful attainment of this objective requires an understanding of the nature of intervention. One of the first goals is to review the background and causes of intervention in developing and developed nations. Only after the objective has been reached can we understand the ways in which nations treat companies differently and the basis of that discrimination.

The final objective of this book is to inject into the discussion of intervention some empirical data, the results of several case studies of subsidiaries, parents and host-nation interventionists and information obtained from discussions with nearly 80 firms and host governments. This is to take the place of the myths and generalizations that appear to litter this field of study.

Coverage

The coverage of the book can be defined in terms of the subject matter dealt with and its applicability to various kinds of nations and companies. The broad subject involved here can be described as *political risk* management. From a corporate decision-making perspective, the subject can be divided into two categories. The first category consists of the collection and assessment of political risk data for the purpose of predicting the general political environment in a particular nation. This is generally called macro-political risk. These risks are general in nature and cover revolutions, other forms of political instability, changes in the nation's power structure and changing alliances from West to East. It is these kinds of risks that most observers refer to when considering political risk. So multinational firms, banks and others spend considerable resources to ensure that they can avoid another occurrence such as Castro's Cuba, Allende's Chile and Khomeini's Iran. (See Kobrin, 1982, for a review of macro-political risk.)

Not all firms suffer equally from these occurrences, however. Some firms may be expropriated because of a revolution, while others are either untouched or suffer only slight reductions in performance. In addition, it appears that intervention often occurs because of normal, stable government processes rather than as a result of political instability. And in both cases a considerable degree of discrimination appears to occur in the practice of intervention.

Because of the discrimination that has occurred and because of the frequent absence of political instability, the focus has shifted to what has come to be called micro-political risk. Micro-political risk is defined as the effect or impact of a politically-backed event on a particular firm. Here the emphasis is not on the nation but on the individual firm.

This book deals with micro-political risks. Macro risks such as revolutions may be more dramatic, but micro risks are more prevalent (Robock, 1971; Hawkins and Mintz, 1976; Kobrin, 1979). Hence they are of more importance to the multinational enterprise, host countries and others interested in the international flow of technology and investment.

An analysis of macro-political risks should permit the interested party to evaluate likely outcomes and estimate the effect on his behaviour. This book also attempts to provide firms with similar abilities in the area of micro-political risks. Unlike most cases of macro risks, however, foreign firms do not have to be quite as passive. Consequently in examining the impact of intervention on the individual firm, this book will evaluate in detail the ability of the firm to control the impact of intervention.

This book has limits in terms of its applicability to firms and nations. Multinational *firms* are not homogeneous, and lessons learned from one need not apply to others. As far as intervention is concerned, firms vary in their political significance, economic impact, flexibility, responsiveness to local conditions and in their technological and managerial expertise and rate of change. As firms differ dramatically on each of these dimensions, comparisons decrease in validity.

Similarly, each nation's behaviour is to a certain extent unique. Political dogmas call for varying levels of government intervention;

political instability creates the need to use foreign firms as a unifying enemy; and a growing and increasingly competent entrepreneurial class calls for less foreign ownership and more local sourcing. Even more important, poor and institutionally under-developed nations often view foreign direct investment more benignly than their richer, more-developed, cousins.

Because of this variation within both firms and nations, books such as this need to consider carefully their coverage, or the extent to which one can generalize from the conclusions and findings presented here. This book would have little relevance to the following types of subsidiaries:

1. representative or sales offices;
2. trading houses with little domestic value-added;
3. insurance, pension, banks and other financial intermediaries;
4. service companies; and
5. project construction.

Other firms, such as those in natural resources, will find that most but not all of the conclusions apply to them. When these exceptions occur they will be noted in the text.

This book's applicability to different nations is somewhat limited by political and legal factors. One's ability to generalize from results presented here decreases somewhat when the nation's constitution and legal structure make it difficult to discriminate against foreign-owned firms, namely, USA; and also when significant government-to-government arrangements, such as aid and bilateral military and trade agreements, inhibit action by the host government against firms from its partner's country. These two conditions generally apply to much of the Western developed world and in particular to the Organization for Economic Co-operation and Development (OECD) nations.

One should point out, however, that while those external factors mentioned above reduce a firm's intervention exposure in most developed nations, many of the concepts developed here nevertheless do apply. For example, France's intervention into the US computer subsidiaries in the 1960s and 1970s, and Canada's intervention into foreign oil companies during the late 1970s and early 1980s, follow the pattern developed in this book.

The nations specifically covered by this book range the spectrum from the newly industrialized nations such as Mexico, Brazil and South Korea all the way down to the institutionally and economically under-developed countries such as Tanzania and Bolivia. The very poor nations such as Chad and Bangladesh would not be included here because of the special case of foreign investment in those nations.

Outline

This book is organized into two parts. Part 1 deals with the nature of intervention and contains five chapters.

Chapter 2 discusses the effect of government intervention on the foreign firm, examining in some detail the longer-run behavioural effects on multinational enterprise. In Chapter 3, I develop the argument which outlines the basis and source of intervention in most nations. The role of interest groups is explained and the concept of relative bargaining power is introduced. Chapter 4 is a major chapter which provides empirical support for conclusions showing how certain corporate characteristics determine one's intervention level. Other oft-mentioned factors which have been shown not to affect intervention are also discussed. Chapter 5 takes the national perspective and discusses how each country's average level and type of intervention is established. The role of political instability is also covered. The final chapter in this section reviews the effects of different corporate political behaviour on the level of intervention experienced.

Part 2 deals with the implications of Part 1 for the management of intervention. Chapters 7 and 8 deal with the management problem at the level of the subsidiary and the parent respectively. These are detailed chapters, which in addition review the role of joint ventures and other forms of international activity in reducing intervention. The proposed policies and actions vary as different kinds of host nations and MNEs are considered. Chapter 9 addresses this impact of country and MNE differences on the management of intervention. Chapter 10 summarizes the book. Finally, a set of problems yet to be resolved is outlined.

PART ONE: THE NATURE OF INTERVENTION

2 THE EFFECTS OF INTERVENTION

The subject of intervention is of importance because its main effect is to create costs for multinational firms. From the intervening nation's perspective, the effect is slightly different. They see it as a re-allocation of the benefits of private foreign direct investment from the multinational parent to the host nation.

The costs of intervention to the foreign firm have direct and indirect elements. The direct and overt element attracts public and corporate attention because of its reduction of profit, sales, and its increase of executive heartburn. Less understood have been the indirect, more subtle, effects. These latter costs arise from the new corporate strategies firms adopt because of actual or threatened intervention. These new strategies often are counter-productive, resulting in reduced long-term profitability and increased risk of intervention.

In this chapter the effects of intervention on both the individual subsidiary and the multinational enterprise's worldwide operation are examined. This analysis is followed by describing the effect on intervention sponsors in the host nation. The latter aspect is important because of its use in helping one understand and predict intervention.

Types of Intervention

The *types of intervention* that take place are numerous and appear to be growing in variety. Not all governments practise each type of intervention and certain types are in vogue one year and unheard of three years later.

An intervention is a policy either prescribed by the host government, or supported by it. An example of the latter could be a statement by, say, an association of manufacturers, calling for a 10 per cent increase in domestic value-added by the toiletries industry. When this obtains public and private political support those foreign firms come under pressure to accede. In most nations, companies have to deal with governments in the normal course of business events. Hence, governments have ample opportunity to pressure firms to accept and implement the wishes of such an association.

A further definition of intervention, in the context of this book, refers to its discriminatory nature. All government action which affects other organizations is broadly called intervention. But from the perspective of the foreign firm, one is interested primarily in those government actions which are selective. Across-the-board actions by governments are frequent. These are generally a function of political and economic factors very different from those causing government actions against particular and foreign-owned firms.

Using these definitions, three sets of interventions can be defined. These are described in Table 2.1.

Table 2.1: Examples of Intervention

Financial	Operating
Foreign exchange availability	Local value-added minimums:
Profit repatriation limits	— own manufacture
Export requirements	— domestic sources
Hard currency debt requirements	Maximum limits on market-share
Price controls	Requirements for local production
Limits on research and management	of a product
fees	Use of local distributors
	Staffing restrictions affecting
	foreigners
General/Strategic	
Ownership limits	
Locus of control	
Nature of business (importance,	
assembler, manufacturer)	
Unilateral contract renegotiations	
Bureaucratic harassment	

Source: Poynter, 1978; Berenbeim, 1983.

These interventions vary in their effect on the subsidiary and its parent's worldwide operation. For the subsidiary, the direct effect is somewhat dependent on the area of operation affected by the intervention. In terms of frequency, the following operational areas are affected in decreasing order of importance (Poynter, 1978, pp. 125, *et seq.*):

1. Financial activities (foreign exchange, prices, repatriation);
2. Employment practices (proportion of foreigners, wage rates);
3. Political (civil service administrative speed, unilateral negotiations);
4. Production and marketing (value-added, export quotas limits to local market-share);
5. Ownership and control;

6. Intra-MNE product flows;
7. Nature of business (e.g. a change from importer to manufacturer).

If one assumes that an existing financial, production or sourcing policy constitutes the optimum condition for the MNE, then any forced departure from existing policies in the above operational areas will have direct and indirect effects on the MNE.

Direct Effects on the Subsidiary

The direct effects of intervention are almost all described in terms of costs to the subsidiary and to the multinational organization. Often the first-order costs of intervention are easily quantified. Forced local sourcing of product components rather than continued use of – cheaper – imported components, forced distribution through specified domestic firms rather than a competitive free-market choice of distribution alternatives, and forced exporting from the host country rather than the previous – cheaper – source are all examples where first-order intervention costs are explicit.

The second-order costs of these interventions are related to the weak financial position these firms are placed in. Take a typical case of intervention where any of the above actions result in either an increase in overall production costs (e.g. due to local sourcing) or, a decrease in sales price (e.g. forced exporting) by 15 to 20 per cent. While the intervention is costly, many subsidiaries can withstand it and still be financially viable, especially when many of the investment costs are already sunk.

Strategic Disadvantages

Strategically, their position is often worse. Because of their reduced profit margins, these subsidiaries find that competitors constitute a greater threat now than before the intervention. Domestic competitors have a better competitive position than before and, depending on the circumstances, are sometimes stronger. Dominant market-shares come under threat, new product introductions become difficult to fund internally, strategic options are reduced and programmes engaged in almost exclusively by foreign firms, such as management training, come under fire. Increased competitive threats also come from imports and domestic substitutes which, because of the subsidiary's increased costs, become more comparable.

Dealing with these threats, subsidiaries find, now calls for greater interaction with the domestic government. This action – rather than strengthening one's competitive position through manufacturing or marketing improvements – becomes necessary simply because of a process of elimination. The effect of intervention is to reduce the flexibility of subsidiary management, and thus has to increase costs. When one is forced to source components locally or export to markets where prices are significantly below the domestic market, there is little management can do to improve its position internally. It turns then, for want of other alternatives, to the host government for assistance with grants and subsidies. Host governments sometimes assist in these situations without some *quid pro quo*. As it does for nationalized industries in most of the developed world, however, this process often marks the beginning of a downward spiral of decreasing competitiveness.

Therefore, while relatively moderate interventions may leave the subsidiary financially viable, it often finds itself in a poor strategic position with fewer options than before. In many situations, strategic flexibility for the foreign-owned subsidiary is a highly desirable advantage to offset the omni-present weakness of the foreign firm: their relative lack of knowledge of the domestic business environment compared to that of local competitors. The reduced control over competitive elements such as cost and market prices which intervention brings also pushes the subsidiary closer to the host government as it tries to maintain its competitive position. In that area, too, the foreign subsidiary is at a decided disadvantage compared to domestic firms.

Local Ownership and Joint Ventures

The costs of forced local ownership and control (*joint ventures*) are more complex to measure. Where local ownership is purchased from the MNE, the direct financial cost is the difference between the price received for the equity share compared to the value of the income stream (mostly dividends) and the value of the assets given up. As most such shareholding is acquired either for a nominal sum or through earned buyouts (using one's share of future dividends to pay for the equity), the cost to the foreign firm is usually high.

The greater cost of forced joint ventures with host-country partners appears to result from their high failure rate after operations have started. Franko (1971), Stopford and Wells (1972), Killing (1982, 1983), Schaan (1983) and Beamish (1984) have pointed out how the popularity of joint ventures owes more to government decree (intervention) and corporate *naïveté* than to the benefits actually derived from this particular form of operation. Many, if not a majority, of joint ventures are unstable or unprofitable. More to the point, it appears that relatively few joint ventures actually reach the goal set by the MNE partner, whether it be joint venture profitability, learning about new markets, or for competitive reasons.

Several observers of joint venture activities have traced the problems to strategic and policy conflicts associated with double parenting (see Killing, 1982, 1983; Schaan, 1983). Partners differ in terms of preferred risk level, dividend payout preferences, need for control of the joint venture, business goals of the venture, purpose of the venture for each partner and the level of integration and differentiation with their parents' operations. When the MNE partner has typical goals of moderate risk, five-year payback, and high market-share, for example, there can be few business strategies shared with a domestic partner wanting low risk, slow growth or market skimming, and a three-year payback on investments. Other conflicts occur when MNE parents use joint ventures to protect foreign markets against other foreign competitors. In these cases profits and dividend payments are seldom up to the level of domestic partner aspirations.

MNE executives are often told by consultants, advisors, authors and government officials that the major way to reduce the costs of forced joint ventures is to pay considerable attention to the task of selecting the 'right partner'. Many of the difficulties MNEs run into through joint ventures, these people say, can be substantially reduced by finding the appropriate partner.

As with requests to be good corporate citizens, many firms have found they have trouble not with the idea of the 'right' partner but with its operational definition. Defining precisely what kind of partner one wants appears to be difficult, uncertain and illustrative of the many trade-offs involved. Should one select domestic partners with weak or strong political connections, with complementary or similar management and technical skills, with substantial financial resources, or a young, poor, firm; or should one join forces with a silent partner or an active, participative one?

MNEs subjected to this most popular form of intervention report that each of these choices involve costs. Partners with strong political ties carry higher risks of greater government requirements to implement even the most unrealistic of government decrees, and the risk of a backlash should the ruling party change. Politically-inactive partners carry their own costs: little help with understanding and predicting policy changes, slow bureaucratic processes and little domestic strength in general to help manage domestic competition. Similarly, partners knowledgeable about the business activity in question know what kind of assistance is necessary to adapt the business to the host country, and can constructively discuss business problems with the MNE. On the other hand, because of their business knowledge, it is precisely these domestic firms which are the fastest to learn how to operate the joint venture without the MNE.

These are a few choices, in other words, which can reduce the costs of the forced joint venture. For many MNEs, either strategic conflicts occur or problems of selecting and managing the domestic partner make this kind of intervention one of the potentially most expensive.

Direct Effects on the MNE Parent

So far we have been examining the costs of intervention on the smallest unit of the MNE, the subsidiary. The MNE parent is affected by intervention in two ways. The first and rather obvious way is the effect on the parent's consolidated financial condition and competitive position as government intervention reduces the subsidiary's profit and net asset position. As many MNEs become more integrated in their operations, intervention disrupts inter-subsidiary flows of products and technology. Firms such as Black & Decker, IBM, ITT, automobile manufacturers and many others increasingly trade finished products and components within the firm because of scale economies, world product mandates and governmental export requirements. These activities call for increased standardization of products and components, and worldwide inventory control. Interventions which require greater domestic production or value-added, product adaptation to local markets, and the presence of local partners who may not view decisions based on maximizing worldwide MNE profits as being in their own local interests, can result in costly adjustments.

For example, subsidiaries in Brazil have to cater to industrial customers demanding up-to-date technology (hence the need to be closely integrated with the parent organization), and must export — frequently to related subsidiaries — to satisfy foreign exchange requirements. When firms are forced to increase their level of Brazilian sourcing they in effect have to arrange for the new Brazilian components to be manufactured to the firm's worldwide standards. Material standards, tolerances and product performance compatible with, say, the MNE's plant in West Germany, have to be replicated in Brazil.

The managerial task of replicating home country performance standards in a developing host country like Brazil is staggering. Most developing nations, Brazil included, operate in a protected market. Managerial attention is not directed towards lowering production costs through effective production techniques, nor at lowering overhead costs, nor watching competitors and quickly responding to competitive or consumer activities. Instead, subsidiary managers have traditionally concentrated on parent-subsidiary administration, managing host government relations, obtaining the desired production output, domestic sales and, to a lesser extent, marketing.

In order to meet these demands of greater exports, subsidiaries have to modify their basic strategy. Domestic executives have to be re-directed and retrained, often at considerable cost and significant level of turnover. Even senior, home nation executives have to be replaced because of the difficulties they have in changing their orientation or changing that of their subordinates. Overall, the process of changing a protected subsidiary into a relatively efficient world-scale producer or manufacturer is time consuming, costly in terms of human resource management problems and, as many firms in Mexico, Brazil, Spain, Nigeria and India will agree, seldom meets expectations.

Direct Benefits of Intervention

So far, the discussion has concerned the dominant negative effects of intervention. However, executives do talk as well about the benefits of intervention. While there undoubtably are some benefits to be derived from acceding to intervention decrees, it appears that this discussion is influenced by two factors:

1. confusion among executives between the notions of 'benefit from intervention' on the one hand, and on the other, the actual cessation of intervention;
2. the low costs of some interventions.

Much intervention appears to occur during short-lived spurts of policy-making or enforcement which may last two or three months and then cease for a year or so. The relative calm following a successful inter-vention can be misleading. This calm is not caused by the acceptance of intervention by the subsidiary and resultant government satisfaction but the timing of intervention *per se.*

Some interventions take place with little cost to the firm. Some of these have a perceived benefit to the host nation which is greater than the actual cost to the firms. Depending on how the firm publically manages this intervention, the net payoff to the firm may be positive. Public offerings of common stock, name changes, hiring more local executives and technical staff and greater training and education programmes usually fit into this category. Alternatively, interventions may reduce profits but from an already very high level and consequently are not perceived by MNE executives as being 'costly'. The first series of interventions enacted by the Brazilians on a relatively unregulated foreign investment community in the mid-1970s would fit this mould.

Finally, there are circumstances which reduce the impact of intervention. These interventions result in a greater share of subsidiary profits or benefits going to domestic groups, but include a commensurate increase in total subsidiary profits as well. While this kind of intervention is frequent in rhetoric and seldom in reality, successful examples would be forced joint ventures where the domestic partner uses his superior local knowledge and contacts to obtain cost reductions in sourcing and production, or improvements in government regulatory matters.

As Chapter 3 will point out, for this 'desirable' form of intervention to occur the domestic interventionist must be aware of the subsidiary's business environment, and must exercise control – and the MNE must allow control – over those areas in which local partners can assist. More often than not one finds that a domestic interventionist is more aware of the domestic political process than of key business problems and opportunities in the subsidiary. Hence, the intervention seldom provides benefits to the subsidiary and instead just results in a reallocation of benefits to the interventionist.

Strategic Effects of Intervention

Intervention can be described as the unilateral changing of the rules under which a subsidiary operates. Many firms see it as essentially unpredictable, wrong and one-sided. Unlike business activities such as competitive actions or changes in consumer behaviour, intervention is viewed as being illegitimate. Executives react to intervention as they would to any unfair action. They become frustrated and often react emotionally and with little thought to the effectiveness of their actions.

Faced with intervention, a company's long-term reaction is often a logical one. MNEs adjust investment strategies to reflect the risk, uncertainty and frustrations of intervention. The desired profit or hurdle rate is increased, and the assets at risk are reduced.

It appears that the usual effect of this logical strategy is opposite to that hoped for by the firms. The high short-term profits, *ceteris paribus*, make the subsidiary more desirable an object for intervention. In addition, the strategy of reducing the assets at risk often results in high-dividend payout levels, and consequent little growth or expansion but a high political profile. It will be argued later that this strategy of asset reduction does not permit the subsidiary to use many of the techniques for managing and reducing intervention. These techniques often call for asset building and expansion. It will be argued that the traditional reaction of increasing the desired return on assets employed is counter-productive, as it increases rather than reduces intervention.

These strategic effects of intervention play a major role in defining the MNE's negative attitude towards investment in nations where intervention is possible. When the predictable business reactions to this major uncertainty of intervention appear to exacerbate and increase the likelihood of intervention, the groundwork for continued poor management of intervention is in place.

Effects on the Interventionists

Because intervention is caused by the sponsorship and political behaviour of several interested domestic groups, it is almost tautologous to say that the general effect of intervention on them is positive. While the subsequent chapter explores the basis of intervention, it is useful to describe here the nature and kinds of benefits that fall to those who create the basis for intervention.

Of the several groups involved in promoting intervention, two stand out: civil servants and their political bosses, and domestic businessmen (either capitalists or their socialist equivalents). The first group's benefits from intervention are often expressed in political, social and national economic terms. If the intervention called for increasing the domestic value-added for a product, then more local employees are hired, trained, pay taxes, spend money on other goods, and will either vote for — or at least not agitate against — the political leaders. Civil servants and politicians also may be influenced by political beliefs which may find satisfaction in intervention.

The second group one finds playing a role in defining and sponsoring intervention policies are domestic businessmen or their socialist equivalents, such as parastatal managers, nationalized industry presidents, etc. Their benefits from intervention are often immediate, positive and almost always exclusively financial. When intervention results in forced expansion, increased exports, greater domestic value-added, or enforced joint ventures, these local businesses and entrepreneurs benefit. Most of those interventions result in greater domestic production and usually increased purchases from the domestic business sector.

Joint ventures and other similar joint activities are sought after by interventionists for rather obvious financial reasons, but also because these kinds of interventions offer the domestic firm an opportunity to acquire managerial, technological and production skills through working with the foreign firm. These skills are then used in manufacturing associated, and sometimes the same, products. So the domestic partner in a chemical feedstock joint venture can get involved in more specialized downstream chemicals. The partner in an automotive tyre venture expands into rubber tiles and other rubber products. Sometimes the joint venture partner establishes his own manufacturing complex – or takes over the existing one – and competes in the export market manufacturing the same product. The results of petrochemical ventures in South Korea, and bicycle and motor-scooter joint ventures in India provide examples of this practice.

Domestic benefits from the more severe kinds of intervention come in somewhat different form. Interventions which severely limit the commercial activities of the foreign firm such as expropriations, closure of business activities to foreign firms, etc. provide significant benefits as domestic businesses fill the gap left by the departing or constrained MNE. Hence, we have a growing domestic consumer goods industry in Indonesia, petrochemical feedstock firms in South Korea and an indigenous oil business in Canada.

There is some dispute concerning whether there is an overall positive benefit to be derived from intervention. Companies and some economists argue that the net overall economic and social benefits of most interventions are negative. They point out – and I illustrated it earlier in this chapter – that firms will reduce their actual and future investment in the face of intervention. In other words, any gains to the host nation from intervention will be more than outweighed by lower overall investment – and re-investment – rates as firms react to interventions.

Other costs of intervention are a function of the efficiency of the –

partially — displaced subsidiary compared to the domestic firm which replaced it. Significant inequalities result in higher product prices, poorer product performance and inferior export performance for any firm using components from the affected firm. Higher dividend payout rates, and a greater concentration of wealth in the hands of politicians and businessmen who prefer to invest overseas are all oft-quoted costs of intervention.

While it may be correct, this long-term calculation of the costs and benefits is a poor predictor of intervention. It is too rational in one sense, and does not take into account the fact that different groups at different times enjoy the benefits, or endure the costs, of intervention. To the civil servant or politico interventionist, the costs of intervention are long term, the benefits are short term. In addition, the costs are likely — for short-lived regimes — to be borne by another political group or, for the civil servants, by future budgets and plans. In the matter of any cost-benefit analysis of intervention, rational social and economic analysis plays a decided second fiddle to the overt and immediate interests of decision-makers.

Summary

The costs of intervention are directly felt on the MNE's bottom line, and indirectly in the subsidiary's strategically disadvantaged position. Most interventions either increase the cost of production, or decrease the sales price. Some interventions, such as forced joint ventures, cause profits to be shared in return for little or no consideration. Subsidiaries weakened by such intervention become more vulnerable to competition (domestic and foreign), and more dependent on host government support. Neither of these conditions generally forecast a desirable future.

Intervention also disrupts the multinational firm's integrated strategy. Intra-MNE sourcing of technology, components and products is affected, as is the sourcing and utilization of capital funds. The freedom of the MNE to design global strategies is constrained, making it susceptible to less constrained global competitors.

The MNE's traditional reaction to intervention creates other, more strategic, costs. Raising profit requirements, reducing asset exposure and belief in the uncontrollability of intervention has the opposite effect: it causes intervention to increase.

The beneficial effects of intervention on its sponsors, supporters, and on the host nation in general are significant and visible. Politicians and civil servants see desired economic policies implemented, their popularity improve and, sometimes, their bank accounts swell – not all illegitimately either. Domestic businessmen benefit by supplanting the MNE, or at least sharing profitably in the subsidiary's activities. The host nation benefits because politicians, civil servants and businessmen do, and because of any additional local value-added that may accrue.

The costs of intervention to the host nation are generally long term, and less visible. All things being equal, intervention decreases foreign direct investment, and speeds up foreign disinvestment. This constitutes a cost to the extent that host-nation firms can partially or fully replace the foreign investor with equally efficient firms. In certain nations, intervention also results in wealth accumulating in the hands of a few domestic shareholders and politicians. Because of their risky positions these people often prefer to invest overseas rather than re-invest in their own countries.

The net effect on host intervention sponsors is almost always positive, immediate and often financial, while costs are diffused and long term. And while that is the case, intervention in the operation of foreign-owned firms is a fact of life in a majority of the world's nations.

3 THE BASIS OF INTERVENTION

What causes governments to intervene in the operations of the MNE subsidiaries? Why does Brazil 'reserve' particular computer products for Brazilian firms, Nigeria force consumer goods subsidiaries into joint ventures and South Korea force US chemical MNEs out of the country altogether? In pursuit of the answer, this chapter examines the basis of intervention.

On one level the behaviour of host nations seems to differ significantly. Canada, Brazil and Indonesia completely exclude foreign involvement by reserving specific businesses, while India and others use forced joint ventures and local value-added controls. Some nations focus on high technology subsidiaries while others on consumer goods. While some interventions produce visible benefits to the host country, others fail to produce any benefit and deter further foreign investment. It is not immediately clear what are the causes of this apparently questionable and variable activity.

A consideration of the host nation provides some suggestions. Nations are not monolithic, or even bipartisan: they are composed of different groups, each of which is intent on maximizing its special interests. As Vernon pointed out, in countries where the economic role of foreign investment is significant, the attainment of these special interests frequently necessitates interference in the operation of foreign-owned firms (Vernon, 1971). These interest groups act either through the government, or, in a minority of cases, intervene directly. The 'interest group' can, of course, be the government itself.

From the perspective of a person interested in understanding and successfully managing intervention, this chapter will examine those who determine intervention policy. Their intervention behaviour will be discussed and classified, and a definition of intervention will be developed. Finally, one of the key concepts used to explain and manage intervention will be introduced: the relative bargaining power of state and multinational firm.

The Intervention Decision

The intervention decision by a host government is rarely made arbitrarily

25

or in an irrational manner. Even the most autocratic and revolutionary of governments are aware of the economic realities as well as the necessity to avoid incurring disfavour with the populace. This is illustrated, for example, by the continued existence and operation of MNE subsidiaries in such dogmatically anti-capitalist locations as Ghadaffi's Libya, post-Selassie Ethiopia, Khomeini's Iran and post-Portugese Mozambique and Angola.

One could postulate that the formulation of the intervention decision must, by its very nature, be considered a political process. Government political leaders may choose to intervene or not to intervene; they also choose the kind of intervention (local value-added regulations, foreign-exchange controls, etc.); and these leaders also determine which firms will be forced to bear the brunt of the intervention. When the intervention decision is viewed in this manner, it becomes clear that knowing the political costs and benefits of specific kinds of intervention are key to an understanding of the subject.

Two sets of factors affect the political cost-benefit analysis of specific intervention:

1. the economic and political environment within which the intervention decision is made; and
2. the presence and power of domestic business and other interest groups, plus any political opposition.

Both these factors bear heavily on the nation's policy choice and will be dealt with in detail. The political and economic environment will be considered first because of its dominant influence over any discussion on this subject. The behaviour of interest groups within this environment will be discussed in the next section.

The Economic and Political Environment

Although links with foreign companies are sought by host governments because of the anticipated economic benefits, it is the economic costs associated with the foreign presence which may assume increasing significance after the initial few years of operation. This change in emphasis is brought about by factors which are fairly well known and do not require a detailed review here.[1] Fundamentally, they derive from the precarious financial condition of most LDCs, and the frequent fiscal problem of the newly-industrialized nations. Politicians then concentrate on minimizing economic costs which are exacerbated by the very visible costs of certain foreign investments. As a result, a high proportion of the discussions concerning the acceptability of specific subsidiaries revolve around these economic costs. The importance of this issue is frequently increased due to the fact that governments and foreign investors, partially because of ideological differences, tend to focus on different costs and benefits, measured according to different yardsticks.

The problems of producing convincing evidence to support host-government accusations, and the presence of frequent inconsistencies in government charges, have not reduced the number of generalizations about the economic costs of foreign direct investment. These charges are levelled at almost all MNEs regardless of their individual circumstances. The desire of politicians to arrive at universal generalizations contributes to the controversy between the two groups and can lead MNEs to ignore most government comments, even the legitimate and serious criticisms.

Perceived costs of foreign investment may have psychological as well as economic overtones. When the foreign enterprise is established in the host country, its presence is sometimes seen as that of a Trojan horse from which outside states can exert their influence on the host nation. This influence is even more strongly felt when the *home* nation stands for unacceptable or competing economic and political ideologies. In response to this threat, government leaders have used the foreign presence as a political football to facilitate the achievement of their own, or their country's, goals, using the concepts of *dependencia* and nationalism.[2] In effect, these two concepts have become psychological platforms from which attacks against a foreign presence of any sort can be mounted. The important by-product of such attacks is the consolidation of the leader's power and the relative cohesion of the populace under the banner of nationalism.

Two other political factors must be included in any overview of the environment: ideology and colonialism. Ideology's role in the formulation of the host policy towards foreign investors is an important one which, in many cases, accounts for what is sometimes seen as irrational behaviour of host leaders. Ideology influences the manner in which the foreign investor is perceived and, as we shall see later, to a large extent determines the goals pursued by interest groups.

While there is considerable variation in the political orientation of the world, in many countries the ideology of the ruling elite and other powerful groups is strongly influenced by Marxist-Leninist dogma.

These governments, even if they have not totally repudiated the capitalistic or enterprise approach to development, are frequently hesitant to accept foreign direct investment. Those which do accept it, generally do so under internal pressure to increase the domestic level of welfare. These pragmatic considerations are of such magnitude that one will find Western bloc MNEs operating in such avowedly Marxist-orientated countries as Yugoslavia, Poland, Algeria, Romania and Tanzania. Yet investors must be aware that in those nations the calculation of the political costs and the benefits of various national policies differs significantly from that expected in countries with a more capitalistic orientation.

The effect of these economies and political factors on a country's policy towards specific MNEs cannot be precisely ascertained. In the aggregate, however, one can observe two opposing forces at work in both countries with socialist and with capitalist orientations. First, there is the *desire* of most political leaders to have control of their countries and economies without responsibility to, or interference from, foreign investors. In the eyes of many socialist-inclined leaders, foreign investors frequently represent possible supporters of opposition groups and possible opponents of government economic policies. Even alliances between the existing regime and foreign investors have been known to frustrate government planning options because of the constraints imposed by dependence on foreign investor support. On the other hand, this desire for control is tempered by the economic development and the growing aspirations and political clout of the populace. It has now been accepted by many political leaders that for the great majority of countries, foreign direct investors facilitate the achievement of economic growth sufficiently to satisfy the increasing demands of the population.

It is the relative strength of these opposing forces, one implicitly calling for a reduction in foreign investment, the other for an increase, that basically determines the macro-intervention environment. Countries with strong socialist leanings will, of course, put a higher cost on the presence of foreign investors, as they usually represent opposing ideologies. At the same time, where the populace or large numbers of the non-ruling elites have expectations of better welfare, leaders generally have to relax their desire for autonomy in order to reduce local opposition. A classic illustration of this is provided by India's recent reversal of its highly interventionist policy due to deteriorating economic and political circumstances.

The resultant national policy towards foreign direct investors, formally stated, vary greatly around the world. But it will be suggested later that when it comes to implementation, behaviour patterns are more similar than different, despite the formal policies.

Host-nation Interest Groups

The second factor affecting the country's intervention policy is the presence and power of domestic business and other interest groups. The country's policy towards foreign investors appears to be determined by the interplay of local groups attempting to maximize their particular interests. An example of this particular approach to understanding a country's policy would be, for example, to suggest that 'exploitation' by MNEs is:

> . . . a policy outcome in which the national interest is clearly not being pursued because domestic actors crucial to the decision-making process are . . . (making concessions) to foreign investors to advance their own private good at the public expense (Moran, 1974).

As mentioned earlier, four broad types of interest groups are considered pertinent to a study of intervention:

1. the ruling political party;
2. domestic capitalists or, in socialist countries, their government equivalents;
3. non-ruling political groups and other potential leaders;
4. the domestic managerial class.

There are several conceptual approaches to the analysis of the behaviour of these groups in formulating the intervention policy. One approach, which has been popularized by Theodore Moran (1974) concentrates on the alliances formed among these groups and the international companies.

Moran suggests that when there is a threat from socialist or left-wing elements within the host nation, there is usually an automatic alliance between domestic capitalists, right-wing political groups and foreign investors. The presence of foreign investors supports an economic and political system preferred by these two domestic groups, protecting them from the emergence of challenging alternative systems. Therefore, as long as the left-wing threat is perceived to be serious — and while the domestic capitalists and their allies remain relatively powerful — foreign subsidiaries usually escape serious harassment.

Because these relationships are not immutable, situations can develop where all of these groups ally themselves against foreign investors. This change can be attributed to the increasing abilities and expectations of the domestic groups as well as to the failure of many MNEs to accommodate such developments. Both the domestic capitalists and the managerial and supervisory classes begin to realize that their interests are no longer served by unreservedly supporting MNEs. These groups gradually become aware that their needs can more readily be satisfied by *forcing their government* to reduce the MNEs' share of investment benefits and to transfer ownership, control and employment to themselves. In other words, their political power can obtain for them greater rewards than those obtained as friends of foreign companies.

This process of 'replacing' the MNE is being stimulated by the increasing business abilities of domestic firms. All things being equal, intervention of the forced joint venture and increased local value-added types will not occur if the cost of placing the activity in a local company's hands is high. As local entrepreneurs, private companies and state-controlled firms become technologically and managerially more able, their disadvantage relative to the ability of the subsidiary falls to a politically-acceptable level. Alliances then increase among domestic businesses and host-government politicians and civil servants for the purpose of replacing parts of the subsidiary's activities with local players.

This steady replacement of the MNE subsidiary by domestic firms can, in certain nations, take on the characteristics of a well produced play. In Brazil, where government-domestic business links are very refined, the government has been reserving particular products for Brazilian-controlled firms at a rate completely determined by the rising abilities of Brazilian firms. In the computer industry, for example, the steady reservation of 8 bit computers, then 16 bit with 8 bit communications, 16 bit with 16 bit communications, and so on, clearly illustrates the process.

Definition of Political Risk and Intervention

The unwanted involvement of governments in the affairs of companies has traditionally been grouped under the term political risk. That is also the extent of agreement among MNEs, consultants, insurance agencies, governments and writers as to what precisely political risk is all about. Consequently, discussions about political risk – and, therefore, any subset of political risk such as intervention – is clouded by uncertainty, lack of concensus, misunderstanding and jargon. In other words, all the trappings of a new body of knowledge.

In the days when the only form of intervention practised by governments was expropriation, things were easier. Complex interventions such as forced joint ventures, local value-added rules and import-export balancing were not often used by governments. In those days, political risk referred to expropriations and nationalizations, and to the coups and political instability that usually preceded such actions.

Government intervention behaviour changed, muddying the waters of political risk analysis as it did. Intervention became more typical of stable nations rather than of coup-ridden leftist-threatened ones. Expropriations decreased drastically, and even coups often arrived without their usual round of nationalizations and MNE-bashing.

In this section, a conceptual model of political risk linking the concepts of political instability, political risk and government intervention will be proposed. The purpose is to come to a better understanding of what constitutes political risks in the 1980s, and to show how the subject of this book – government intervention – relates to political risk.

Intervention: Politics or Economics?

The main questionable assumption of the traditional approach to political risk is that the political environment is distinct from the business and economic environment. While this may be so in the abstract sense, the interrelationships are so prevalent and strong as to render the distinction useless for practical purposes. A visit to any random selection of nations will show how economic realities impinge on political dogma, philosophy and policies. Equally, most business and economic environments are seldom untouched by regulation, political preference and government support (see Hirschman, 1967; Parvin, 1973).

Host governments argue that many of their domestic policies towards foreign direct investors are attempts to advance domestic industrialization and hence divorced from 'politics'. The foreign investor, on the other hand, views the same policies in light of nationalist economics and the political philosophy of the rulers. Consequently, the MNE interprets their implementation as an example of a 'political' risk.

The distinction between politically or economically induced 'risks' fades further when one examines what appear to be largely economic-based policies. As will be explained further in this book, governments discriminate among firms when they intervene, with the discrimination occurring frequently at the implementation stage when specific firms are actually forced to obey the rules. It is at the implementation stage that economic-based policies become politicized. Such avowedly economic policies as exchange controls are seldom enforced equally among all firms, domestic or foreign. The determination of which firms should bear the brunt of the controls, the timing and the method of exchange controls, is almost always politically influenced. An examination of recent exchange controls in Brazil, India, Mexico and 1982 France provides many illustrations.

I contend that the political and business/economic environments are so intertwined that for firms and analysts to try and disaggregate them is counter-productive. This is especially so in less-developed nations when government involvement in business is, for rather obvious reasons, greater than in developed nations.

Examining the situation from the perspective of the foreign investor rather than the political scientist cum management academic provides some guidance towards a useful perspective. Firms are concerned with any factor which will require or force change in their policies, operations, or characteristics. Some of these factors which force change are inherent in the business environment: competitive actions which force the price of a product down and increases in raw material costs, are both examples where the political input is usually small or non-existent. On the other hand, the political content in a multitude of other factors such as joint venturing, export rates, exchange controls, etc. is high.

It is those factors with the significant political content that are of interest in this discussion, factors which affect operation, policies and characteristics without regard to source, but with a significant political input influencing the ultimate effect on the firm.

Policies in any organization are determined by the interplay of the major interest groups and their environment. These groups affect each other and make decisions in a manner that can be called political process. The regular functioning of this political process results in individuals in these groups evaluating the costs and benefits of intervention, both in a general sense and as far as particular firms are involved. The policy or strategy which evolves can be modelled in the same way as any strategy emanating from a diverse organization.

The policy outcome is a product of the preferences of one particular group, such as the ruling party, and its power *vis à vis* the others. Here, the group's preferences include its goals, tactics and policies. With these preferences and the relative power of each significant group fixed in place, government policy is the outcome of this systematic, relatively stable, decision-making process.

Political Risk versus Intervention Risk

Following these premises, I contend that political risk analysis per se should address *changes* in the decision-making process above. Such analysis would concentrate on three main items:

1. changes in those groups or individuals involved in the decision-making process;
2. the preferences of each of those groups; and
3. their relative power.

Political risk would then be defined as changes in the political process through which decisions affecting firms are made.

Under this approach, a large political risk would describe significant changes in the normal decision-making political process. This would follow a coup or electoral defeat, for example, which would result in significant reshuffling of those groups playing a major role in the decision-making process. Even in this situation there is considerable variation: the radical change of regime in Iran from the Shah's to Khomeini's, for example, compared to a change such as that from Schmidt to Kohl in West Germany in 1982. Smaller risks would result from a re-ordering of the power of particular domestic industrialists or of influential civil servants.

Political risk analysis would also review how the preferences of each major group change over time. This is the most likely and prevalent cause of variation − and hence political risk − in the outcome of the decision-making process. The preferences of these groups, like the strategy of an organization, are affected by four general factors (Andrews, 1980):

1. *environmental*: including competition from other groups and nations; and political, social and economic aspects;
2. *resources* internal to the group: strengths and weaknesses relative to competing groups;
3. *values* of the key actors;
4. *organizational relationships* within the group affecting both the development and execution of the group's preferences or strategy.

Under this formulation of political risk, government intervention is the outcome of the decision-making process described above. While political risks refer to changes in how the political process works, intervention risks refer to the outcome and the effect on the particular firm. For these reasons intervention risk is defined as:

> The probability that a government will enforce policies which will force change in the operations, policies, and strategies of the foreign investor; and the magnitude of the forced change required.

In this sense, a government-enforced policy refers to a decision made by an individual or group of individuals with a power of a nation-state behind it. It does not matter for the purpose of this definition whether the decision was initially motivated by political or economic factors. It was argued earlier that even those government actions which are induced by economic considerations, such as foreign-exchange controls, have a strong political input. The severity of the controls, their scope and discriminatory enforcement are all influenced by the political consequences of various alternative decisions or policies.

This formulation of intervention based on forced change by firms takes into account not only all types of intervention, but also the discrepancy between the firm's present operations, policies and strategies, and those required by the host government. Therefore, this definition results in an estimate of intervention risk that is particular to either the individual firm, or firms with similar characteristics. So, for example, two electronic assembly firms, one a joint venture, and the other a wholly-owned subsidiary, would likely have different assessments of the intervention risks in 1975 Brazil. Likewise, an intervention policy concerning local value-added may be a serious risk to one kind of company but not to another.

These formulations of political risk and intervention risk run counter to, or at least question, traditional views of the subject of political risk. They de-emphasize the concentration on sudden changes in the political environment, and move instead to the discussion of political process rather than events. The accent on high-profile, dramatic government actions is no longer warranted. This is because most political risks are more subtle and more often a result of changes in the preferences of the influential interest groups, rather than the consequence of radical changes in the group's make-up. Similarly, the outcome of this political decision-making – intervention – is more often the hallmark of stability rather than instability.

In addition, political (not intervention) risk as defined here does not differ from firm to firm. It describes changes in a political process over time. Intervention risk, on the other hand, is always firm-specific. It refers to a policy outcome which forces change in the particular subsidiary or its MNE parent. As we shall see, few intervention decrees are universal in enforcement, as compared to their formulation.

Finally, previous concepts of political risk excluded events which were predictable or continuous (see Robock, 1971; Root, 1972, 1976; Haendel, West and Meadow, 1975). It was argued that gradual changes in the environment that were not difficult to predict accurately should not be defined as a political risk. It would seem that to define an area of study or analysis in terms of one's ability to predict carries with it many opportunities for confusion and further misunderstanding. For politically-aware French MNEs, few things would constitute political risks, while the opposite would hold for politically-inexperienced US MNEs.

Other writers have recently re-examined the subject of political risk, some moving in the general direction taken here. Stephen Kobrin (1982) defines political risk as a combination of both political and intervention risks. Instead of forced change, he speaks of 'significant management contingencies', which introduce the additional concept of managerial uncertainty (pp. 29, *et seq.*). These contingencies are generated by 'political events and processes'. Kobrin appears to group both changes in the political decision-making process, together with the effect on each firm, as political risk. (See, for example, Kobrin, p. 32.) Using the concepts developed in this book, Kobrin's definition covers two distinct kinds of risk: change in the nature of the political process, and forced change in firms because of outcomes of the political process. Kobrin in other parts of his book provides several examples of how these are distinct from each other (pp. 36, 39).

The Nature of Intervention

The introductory chapter mentioned how the nature of intervention has changed, with the dominant form being localization measures such as ownership, local content rules and control over repatriation rates. All the groups with a vested interest in intervention have a common goal: to increase their share of the benefits generated by the MNE subsidiary. This goal can be attained either by totally *replacing* the MNE in the subsidiary's operations, or by *sharing* in the subsidiary's benefits while the MNE is still involved.

The 'replacement' outcome occurs during expropriation, nationalization and forced sale or abandonment of the subsidiary. This type of intervention is risky to the interventionist because of the higher likelihood of business failure due to the complete absence of MNE-supplied managerial and technical skills.

Examples of the 'sharing' outcome would be government-enforced joint ventures, domestic public shareholders, local product or component sourcing, product distribution through a domestic firm, hiring quotas, etc. The sharing type of intervention is the more prevalent type found in most nations since the late 1960s.

Types of Intervention

Consequently, one can define intervention as practised by most nations as forced sharing of the benefits (economic mostly) generated by the subsidiary. When viewed this way, interventionists have two means of increasing their share. As Figure 3.1 illustrates, Type 1 intervention occurs when interventionists profit by increasing the *total* benefits generated by the subsidiary, holding each party's share constant. Type II intervention is more costly to the MNE and more prevalent: domestic interventionists increase their share of the benefits without any overall improvement in the economic performance of the subsidiary.

To the MNE and its subsidiary Type I intervention is preferable. Many firms and governments historically thought of this outcome when joint ventures were established and domestic sourcing and exporting were first considered. Here, each group contributes the skills and technology appropriate to the venture, arriving at a somewhat idyllic state of synergetic match. Although infrequent, Type I intervention does occur. For example, forced joint ventures and government business arrangements in the petroleum and mining sectors often constitute satisfactory and even desirable interventions. Host-government grants and subsidies — also interventions — are of the Type I variety. Governments offer them to induce desired corporate behaviour.

This book is concerned with Type II interventions, where domestic interests are increased at the direct cost of the MNE's share. Few MNE subsidiaries experience desirable Type I intervention, others experience moderately costly Type II, while still others find the intervention level to be so high that operations have to be discontinued or dramatically reduced. In the next chapter we will examine the causes of this varied experience among the operations of multinational enterprises.

Figure 3.1: Types of Intervention

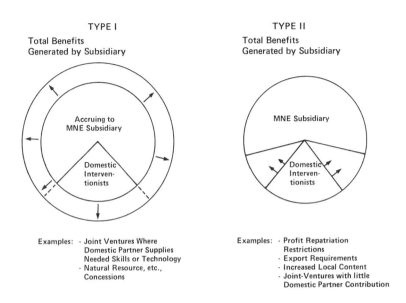

Intervention Variation

Before we examine the causes of high and low levels of intervention, one other characteristic of intervention should be reiterated in order to place the following two chapters in context. Observation and research on a selection of nations (Poynter, 1978) strongly suggests that intervention variation within a nation is high. Traditionally, one felt that judicious selection of a particular country for investment guaranteed a low level of intervention. So firms went, say, to the Philippines expecting little forced intervention, and to Tanzania expecting the opposite. It is contended that these generalizations are strategically misleading and suggest inappropriate investment strategies. Observation strongly suggests that in most cases there is as much variation of intervention experiences within most nations as there is variation among nations.

Subsequent chapters will show how interventionists and their governments discriminate when they formulate and enforce intervention policies. Certain firms experience considerable intervention and others experience little. Furthermore, the basis of the discrimination is not completely determined by the broad business sector of the firm.

It appears that the eye of the interventionist evaluates more than just the industry sector in deciding to press for intervention.

If this view of intervention behaviour is correct, then the emphasis on the *average* levels of intervention in each country, as a basis for selecting investment sites or risk levels, is misplaced. Instead, emphasis should be placed on the intervention exposure of each subsidiary. This book shall argue that the absolute intervention exposure of each subsidiary plays the greater role in determining the level of intervention, not country selection. In other words, subsidiary characteristics are the determining factor, not host-nation characteristics or policies.

Notes

1. Strenuous efforts by host governments to reduce foreign exchange outflows are one of the prime indicators of this change in emphasis. In addition to the incentives for governments to focus on the damaging effects of foreign exchange imbalances, governments also begin to concentrate on costs because of their increased bargaining power once the foreign enterprise has been established and is operating smoothly, viz. Brazil. See, for example, Stephen Hymer's work on bilateral monopolies in *The International Operations of National Firms* (MIT Press, Cambridge, MA., 1977).

2. The *dependencia* theorem states that by accepting foreign direct investment from a major nation, host nations will increase their technological and cultural dependency on the *home* countries. The struggle against dependencia is based on the desire to restore sovereignty and independence over the course of national development. See, for example, Theodore H. Moran, *Multinational Corporations and the Politics of Dependence: Copper in Chile* (Princeton University Press, Princeton, 1974) p. 7.

4 CORPORATE DETERMINANTS OF INTERVENTION

What causes the different intervention experiences of MNE subsidiaries within the same nation? In pursuit of this answer, it was found that concentrating on the specific characteristics of each subsidiary was a fruitful activity.

Multinational enterprises – like nations – differ in their organizational structures, strategies and characteristics (Stopford and Wells, 1972). Firms organize by geographic area or by product line; have autonomous subsidiaries; use their overseas subsidiaries as part of a globally integrated strategy; produce complex, changing products in a price conscious market; or mature, relatively uncomplex products where successful marketing is the key. Upon evaluation of these company characteristics in light of their intervention experiences, one is better able to see the relationships between subsidiary characteristics and their intervention experiences. This allows better understanding and predictability of each firm's intervention rate.

This chapter will introduce the major determinant of intervention – bargaining power – and relate it to specific characteristics of the subsidiary. I will then evaluate other characteristics, such as company size and strategic significance, which also appear to affect intervention. Finally, I will examine those often mentioned characteristics which, in fact, appear not to influence the behaviour of interventionists. The national determinants of intervention are discussed in Chapter 5.

The Concept of Bargaining Power

One of the basic tenets of the theory of intervention is that intervention is fundamentally determined by the activities of various domestic interest groups. Local businessmen, executives in government-owned enterprises, civil servants and politicians would all press the government to enact or support intervention when these groups singly or in collaboration could benefit from such action.

Intervention takes place, then, against those subsidiaries where the intervention sponsors would expect to realize a net positive benefit. Interventionists select subsidiaries by estimating the benefits from intervention in both economic and political terms.

Economic Benefits from Intervention

It appears that the main economic criterion used by interventionists as they discriminate among the available set of subsidiaries is the importance of the MNE-owner to the continued success of the subsidiary. Or in other words, the ability of the domestic interventionist to operate the subsidiary successfully without the co-operation of the MNE.

It is generally agreed that one of the best means of evaluating this net benefit from intervention is to consider the relative bargaining power of the foreign investor as compared with the bargaining power available to the interventionists. Here, the MNE's bargaining power is based on scarce resources the firm can make available, *relative* to resources available either within the host nation or from other, external sources.

These scarce resources are defined as those required to make the subsidiary successful. They can be divided into two groups: those usually under the control of the MNE, and those controlled by the host nation. As will be explained later in this chapter, the resources usually supplied by the MNE include product and process technology, managerial skills, capital, access to export market, etc. Host governments, on the other hand, control access to their internal market, raw materials, labour, sometimes capital, etc. It is generally agreed that MNEs with low bargaining power – relative to the resources of both the host nation and domestic competition – often experience more costly intervention than MNEs with relatively high bargaining power. Host nations with few of the MNE's skills tend not to intervene because of historic lack of success in replacing the MNE and successfully operating the subsidiary. For those interventionists the costs of intervention outweigh the benefits.

Political Benefits from Intervention

However, not all the potential intervention sponsors measure the costs and benefits of intervention exclusively in economic terms. Domestic politicians and civil servants include social and political gains from intervention. Firms in the natural resources sector will point to these non-economic benefits as constituting the main determinants of intervention in those strategically important industries.

Those mostly political benefits will be outlined in the last section of this chapter. First, we will examine those factors which appear to determine the interventionists' perception of their relative bargaining power and hence their desire to intervene: the characteristics associated with the MNE subsidiary.

The Company Determinants of Bargaining Power: the General Theory

Overall bargaining power is determined by who has control over, or access to, factors which are perceived to influence the continued success of the subsidiary in question. Because we are looking at the company determinants in this chapter, we will first look at the question of which corporate factors are core to the firm's success, then at the question of control, and finally the role of perceptions.

Core Activities

As every student of corporate strategy knows, firms do not place equal emphasis on all aspects of their activities. Every firm owes its success to several key activities which it needs to perform well in order to succeed. These may be marketing, cost control, or exporting, access to the latest technology, or any combination of these and many others. These core activities vary among firms but generally, the specifics of one's industry play a role in determining which activities of the firm must be core activities.[1] So, for example, firms in the consumer-packaged goods field (cereals, toothpaste, etc.) concentrate on having excellent marketing rather than excellent production. Both are desirable, but the former is a competitive requirement.

In addition to the above, subsidiaries may have other activities which are the key to their success. In many developing countries it is the ability to carry out complex manufacturing or managerial tasks in an economically and institutionally under-developed nation, or to be a successful exporter, or — through the MNE parent — to have rapid access to new technologies or skills. Identifying these core activities constitutes the initial step in determining the firm's exposure to intervention.

Control

The bargaining strength of all these core activities is determined by who has control over the resources or skills required for the activity. The production of pressurized metal containers — such as aerosol cans — requires the skills to procure, operate and maintain rather complex machinery, and purchasing skills which will deliver the right raw materials at the appropriate times. In many nations, these skills are not readily available and hence under the control of the MNE, giving the MNE a high level of bargaining power. The same would not hold true for the production of, say, toothpaste tubes or non-pressurized, multiple-seam cans, and other uncomplex products requiring less-advanced skills. These skills are more likely to be available, and more easily learned, in a majority of host nations.

Similar situations occur in developed countries, but at a much higher level of skill complexity. As an illustration, the prominent role played by US, UK and French oil companies in Canada's active exploration activities during the 1970s was possible only because at that time Canada did not have the frontier oil exploration skills and the large amounts of risk capital necessary. Consequently, these foreign oil firms had considerable bargaining power, and this was reflected in their economic performance and lack of costly intervention during that period.

The ability of the subsidiary to manufacture a product efficiently, or to procure and keep export markets, provides little bargaining power should domestic firms be able to perform those tasks. Historically, subsidiaries and their MNE parents were almost exclusive suppliers of product technology, marketing know-how and management skills. In the past, even if one of the subsidiary's core activities was the low-cost, somewhat complex, manufacturing of an electro-mechanical product there would be few, if any, other parties interested in providing the same skills. From the perspective of an aspiring interventionist, the bargaining power of that subsidiary was high: the skills required to operate the firm were high and because no other sources of these skills were readily available, the MNE effectively controlled access to them.

Alternative sources of these core skills have increased over the last decade or two. There are a number of private, governmental and multilateral consulting groups who provide technological, marketing and management assistance. At the same time, the increasing number of MNEs from countries such as India and South Korea, and growing competition among traditional MNEs, has allowed interventionists to aquire more easily the skills needed to operate subsidiaries successfully.

Consulting firms, trading houses and other MNEs have been known to replace the previous owners in many subsidiaries. Moreover, the awareness among aspiring interventionists that one particular MNE no longer has a monopoly over the supply of core skills has increased their confidence that somehow they can acquire the necessary skills. Hence the amount of intervention has increased commensurately.

An excellent illustration of this process of replacing the MNE with other suppliers of core skills is provided by the Brazilian computer industry. In several Brazilian operations I've visited they obtain:

1. general management and marketing assistance from a choice of management consultants in the US, England and Germany;
2. production expertise from Japanese engineering consultants and producers of assembly and testing equipment;
3. complex components such as stepper motors for disc drives from small specialist manufacturers in the US and England;
4. microprocessors and other digital chips from sources ranging from major US producers such as Intel down to 47th Street, New York, jobbers and wholesalers.

Traditionally only MNEs were able to supply all or most of these skills – and the output, components – thereby providing the MNE with control.

Perceived versus Actual Power

The final factor affecting the company's relative bargaining power is the role of perceived versus actual bargaining power. The explanation of intervention is substantially the explanation of group behaviour. While economists and businessmen may argue about the precise core activities of a subsidiary, and exactly how much of a gap exists between domestically available skills and those necessary to operate the subsidiary, the often inexact perceptions of outside groups are the motivating factors in any intervention. As will be explained in Chapter 6, foreign firms can, of course, directly influence these perceptions in the MNE's favour. However, outside of these direct manipulations of interest groups' perceptions, their opinions are drawn from often brief and superficial examination of the subsidiary in question.

The fact that intervention decisions are based on sometimes misleading perceptions acts in some firms' favour and against others. Industry stereotypes arise in people's minds and are often at odds with the realities. The manufacture of footware, for example, is often thought of as being relatively uncomplex, and hence within the grasp of most nations and domestic firms. This perception provides subsidiaries with little bargaining power. As many rash interventionists have found out, the efficient manufacture of footware requires high managerial and manufacturing skills. Accurately forecasting material flows is a core activity because the product does not lend itself to having parts retrofitted. Cement manufacture would be another example of an industry suffering from false perceptions of requiring relatively simple technology and few managerial skills.

Other kinds of industries give the impression of requiring more competence than actually necessary. The fabrication of plastic containers and most metal-working activities would fall into this category.

An Illustration: Bargaining Power in Argentina

To illustrate the general theory of bargaining power and intervention Figure 4.1 contains a sample list of subsidiaries and the likely range of their bargaining power in a country such as Argentina. A range of likely bargaining power levels is mentioned because of the flexibility possible within each product category.

Figure 4.1. Bargaining Power by Product Category

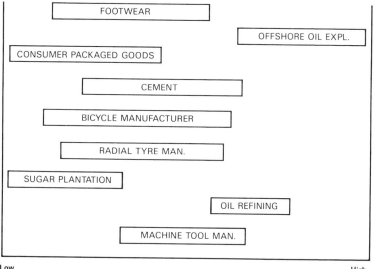

MNE BARGAINING POWER

In summary, then, it has been suggested that the level of intervention experienced by each subsidiary is determined to a large extent by that subsidiary's bargaining power. The amount of bargaining power in the MNE's hands is defined by how much it contributes to, or controls access to, the success of the core activities of the subsidiary.

Because intervention is caused by individuals and groups, perceptions play an influential role in identifying the core activities, in evaluating the MNE's contribution to successful operations and its control over alternative suppliers of the required skills.

The Corporate Determinants of Bargaining Power: Practice

In spite of the seeming complexity of this intervention process, decisions to intervene are made. Recording the level of intervention experienced by firms and comparing it to their corporate policies, operations and characteristics confirms the bargaining power model. We are also directed towards those key corporate characteristics which ultimately influence intervention activities.

Several research projects since the mid-1970s have arrived at substantially similar conclusions concerning the more influential corporate determinants of intervention. (See Bradley, 1977; Poynter, 1978, 1982; Kobrin, 1980; Fagre and Wells, 1982; Lecraw, 1984[2].) I examined the intervention experiences of over 130 subsidiaries and found that four company characteristics in particular played the major role in determining perceptions of their bargaining power and hence their level of intervention. They are as follows:

1. the operational and managerial complexity inherent in the subsidiary;
2. the proportion of foreign nationals in managerial and technical positions;
3. the amount of sourcing with affiliated companies;
4. company exports.

With the exception of the factor dealing with managerial positions, these were all positive determinants of intervention. In other words, high complexity, large amounts of intra-MNE sourcing and a high amount of exports all increased the subsidiary's bargaining power and subsequently reduced the amount of intervention experienced. These four sets of company characteristics will now be explained in some detail.[3]

Operational and Managerial Complexity

The corporate characteristic with the greatest influence over the level of intervention experienced is the operational, technical and managerial complexity inherent in the operation of the subsidiary. In the operational sense, complexity refers to the level of skills required to operate the subsidiary. In the managerial sense, complexity refers to the number, difficulty and interrelationship of managerial decisions required to produce a product.

There is considerable variation among firms in terms of complexity. Some process operations such as found in petrochemicals not only require complex machinery, highly trained operators and problem-solvers, but also need the relationships among all the individual stages of production to be co-ordinated and modified if departures from the norm occur. Other activities, say, the manufacture of plastic containers, are essentially single stage and utilize easily understood and maintained machinery. Finally, markets can be dynamic or stable and competition can be only in terms of cost, or involve all the functional areas of business.

The significance of the complexity factor can be readily observed in many of the advanced LDCs such as Kenya, Indonesia, Brazil, etc. There is considerable local pressure on those governments to hand over to local control uncomplex subsidiaries such as those in consumer goods retailing, importing and exporting, distribution, etc.: firms with few inherent incentives for maintaining the foreign connection. This process is well advanced in countries such as India and recently Nigeria, which have institutionalized the transfer to local control of foreign subsidiaries which are considered '. . . critical to indigenization . . .' (*Business Week*, 1976). Under the 1977 Phase II controls announced in Nigeria, the '. . . smallest and least sophisticated foreign companies . . . must be 100% Nigerian', while those using 'some' foreign input will be 60 per cent Nigerian, and those 'heavily dependent on imported skills' only had to be 40 per cent locally owned (*Business Week*, 1976).

While the specific manner in which firms can estimate their own level of complexity is discussed in Part 2 of this book, a few comments may be useful in clarifying some issues. One is speaking here exclusively of the complexity involved in operating the subsidiary and not the parent MNE. Some subsidiaries look at the high R&D intensity of their parent firms, for example, and believe that the subsidiary is equally complex. MNEs are almost always multi-product companies, making it difficult to generate statements about each subsidiary based on the MNE's worldwide activities. ITT may have extensive R&D and may overall engage in complex manufacturing and managerial activities, but in some subsidiaries they also produce far less complex products, such as prepared foods.

Not surprisingly, the complexity factor appears to be the most powerful of the ingredients in determining the firm's bargaining power. While its role is straightforward and relatively uncomplicated, we shall see in Chapter 7 that implementing a strategy of maintaining the perception of complexity over time is difficult and complicated.

Foreign Nationals in Senior Subsidiary Positions

The significance of this factor was a somewhat surprising finding until one views it as a powerful ingredient in determining people's perceptions of operating and managerial complexity. In this context, this characteristic is a surrogate for the level of complexity: all things being equal, the greater the complexity of the subsidiary, the more reliant the firm becomes on foreigners to staff complex positions. To the domestic interventionist, therefore, a large proportion of foreigners suggests greater complexity and hence greater bargaining power in the hand of the MNE.

As suggested earlier, the relationship between the number of foreigners and intervention is not straightforward. Figure 4.2 shows how the relationship is apparently U-shaped.

Few foreign nationals in the subsidiary suggest little complexity, with a resultant poor intervention experience. As the proportion of foreigners grow, intervention falls as expected. The interesting aspect is the unexpected *increase* in intervention as the proportion of foreigners rise over 50 per cent.

In looking for an explanation of the U-shaped relationship, one tends to find a ready explanation in the negative host-nation attitudes towards foreign firms with a dearth of local managers. Governments tend to be quite negative towards such a flagrant refusal to train and use local staff. Furthermore, the subsidiary's political profile is raised because of its implicit statement about the competency of local staff. Finally, with the subsidiary's constant need for visas and work permits, the host government has more opportunities to intervene in the firm's operations than it would have otherwise.

Sourcing with Affiliated Firms: Vertical Integration

Another means of increasing bargaining power is the MNE's control over products purchased from and sold to associated firms. It appears that the existence of this external control over intra-MNE trade acts as a deterrent to host intervention, the MNE's strength being a function of the volume of these 'tied' sales or vertical integration. In this situation, a frequently mentioned example of a subsidiary with a high degree of defensive ability would be an electronics firm, using semi-finished inputs from an associated firm, and exporting still semi-completed products to another associated firm.

Because of the increased competition among traditional MNEs, and new MNEs from Japan and other countries, this means of improving bargaining power is increasingly subject to attack. Consultants, trading houses and other firms offer alternative access to markets and sources of components. Classically, interventionists were loath to act against subsidiaries involved in intra-MNE sourcing out of fear that they could not find other parties to replace the MNE links. The situation has changed somewhat, with the strength of this particular factor being influenced by the uniqueness of the product or component sourced and the availability of compatible alternatives. While the size and scope may not make it a perfect analogy, the intervention of OPEC in the major oil companies is a good lesson in how the power of intra-firm sourcing can be negated.

Figure 4.2: Staffing Policy and Intervention

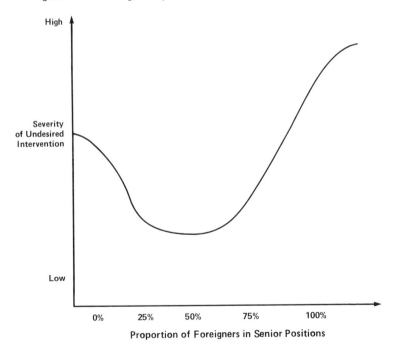

Exports

While it is not surprising that sales to affiliated firms provide subsidiaries with an increase in effective bargaining power, it has been found that exports *in general* also have a similar effect. The relationship between exports and intervention was not, however, a linear one: as firms started to export, intervention also *increased*, but subsequently decreased when the amount of exports became significant to the host nation. The small and medium-sized firm enjoyed significantly less intervention than a firm serving just the local market only after exports exceeded approximately 40 per cent of sales. Larger firms can expect the minimum proportion of exports necessary to produce a reduction in intervention to be smaller. But small, token gestures in exporting almost always seem to have the effect opposite to what many exporting novices had hoped would occur.

Summary

In summary it has been found that when the subsidiary has high relative bargaining power, it can expect little costly intervention as compared to other foreign-owned firms in a particular nation. It is this factor that is the fundamental explanation for intervention and not nationality, size, business activity and all others traditionally suggested by observers.

Neither is intervention unpredictable or unexplainable. That is not to say there are no unpredictable elements or chance, but that those elements no longer dominate the discussion.

One should remember that firms with a high level of bargaining power, such as the highly integrated, complex operation of some of ITT's divisions, not only constitute protection against extreme cases of intervention (e.g. replacing ITT's subsidiary), but also against cases of forced and costly sharing of subsidiary profits (e.g. joint ventures, local sourcing, etc.). Because continued ITT involvement in a particular subsidiary's operations is necessary for the subsidiary's success, the possibility of the MNE reducing that involvement deters intervention. MNEs can also deter forced joint ventures, etc. by taking profits from the threatened subsidiary to another subsidiary (product transfers, royalties, etc.); by serving export markets with other subsidiaries; and in the expreme case by systematically transferring production to other subsidiaries.

In other words, the MNE can threaten to reduce the size of the economic 'pie' in host nations where intervention is considered, transferring the benefits (profits) to other subsidiaries where possible. On the other hand, subsidiaries with less bargaining power will find that the continued involvement of the MNE is less important to the formers' success, and hence their threat of retaliation is less effective in countering intervention.

One must also be careful here to distinguish between those subsidiaries which appear desirable to interventionists, and those which actually experience high levels of intervention. While high technology subsidiaries may be more attractive to host-nation interventionists because of their typically larger profits and growth prospects, they do not automatically experience higher intervention. Instead, less complex and less integrated firms, such as those involved in household toiletries, experience greater intervention. Applying the bargaining power model, one can see that the higher intervention in household toiletries is not because of their profits (often lower than those of more technical firms) but because of the ability of local interventionists to operate the subsidiary without the assistance of the MNE.

Other Company Influences over Intervention

While bargaining power and the factors that constitute or define it substantially determine a subsidiary's intervention exposure, there are other influences which play a less significant, but none the less important, role. Unlike bargaining power, most of these influences are not easily modified by the firm and hence have little impact on one's ability to manage intervention. These influences are:

1. the size of the subsidiary and its impact on the local economy;
2. the strategic importance of the subsidiary to the host nation;
3. the role of industry type.

Impact

There have been two opposing schools of thought concerning the effect the company's impact has on the level of host intervention. The more popular opinion states that large companies attract greater attention and intervention because of their economic significance and high visibility, combined with their inadvertent role as representatives of a foreign, wealthy nation.

The alternative view, while recognizing the host's inclination to intervene in dominant companies, states that due to the company's size, host nations perceive large companies to be too difficult to digest, manage and compensate (Gasser and Rossier, 1974; Truitt, 1970). It is argued that such difficulties outweigh any apparent political advantages that may accrue to domestic interest groups. Host-government spokesmen are also ambiguous about the desirability of large firms.

As one attempts to evaluate the effect of a firm's impact on intervention, one realizes there are several choices in measuring the impact of a subsidiary. Arguments can be made for using assets, sales, or employees as indicators. The author's work has shown that while there is a positive correlation between measures of assets and sales and the extent of government intervention, these are not the most significant. It is the number of employees that seems to play the largest role (Poynter, 1978; 1982). Firms with a large number of employees appear to experience more costly intervention than do firms with few employees. The exact breakpoint between large and small employers is difficult to determine, but 75 or 50 employees appears to be a good indicator.

Subsidiary managers indicate that this relation comes about because of the role played by politicians and trade union officials. Apparently, it is only when the employment level reaches approximately 75 or 50 that labour unions and political parties tend to become quite interested in organizing the workers. This involvement with the unions and politicians, say executives, increases their exposure to government localization measures such as greater local production, more exports, more local managers, etc. Normally firms deal with an isolated bureaucrat concerning these localization matters. Once the workers are organized, however, their union leaders have a vested interest in forcing both their government and their employer to speed up localization. So significant is this factor, that executives in several countries are frequently willing to forego profitable expansion plans in order to avoid the disadvantages of increased employment.

Strategic Importance

Those readers familiar with intervention will not at all be surprised that almost without exception multinational subsidiaries which operate in an area of strategic importance to the host nation experience greater intervention. A strategic industry in this sense is defined as one which is critical to the political and economic development of the host nation. This would include steel makers, oil refiners and the natural resource segment, as having the biggest strategic significance. Examples of firms with little strategic importance would include those in most consumer goods activities, container manufacturers, electro-mechanical firms, etc.

The political philosophy of the ruling regime also influences the definition of a strategic industry. Although there is only little data to support this (see Poynter, 1978), I contend that the socialist countries have a greater tendency to define medium to large employers as strategic industries without regard to their industrial activity.

The reason for the high intervention rates of strategic companies are straightforward and similar to those facing large subsidiaries. Strategic companies have a high political profile which places them near the centre of most political activities. Added to this presence is the use of foreign firms as a rallying bogeyman by politicians. Hence the political – as compared to economic – benefits to be derived from intervention into these firms is higher. Firms operating in these sectors expect intervention and, as will be pointed out in Part 2, resort to very different management techniques to handle the problem.

By combining a firm's strategic importance and its bargaining power one can begin to understand a firm's overall exposure to intervention. Figure 4.3 illustrates the relationship for a selection of product categories. Intervention is likely upwards and to the right of the dotted line. The specific location of this line is determined by the bargaining power of each nation and its sensitivity towards strategic industries.

Figure 4.3: Bargaining Power, Strategic Importance and Intervention

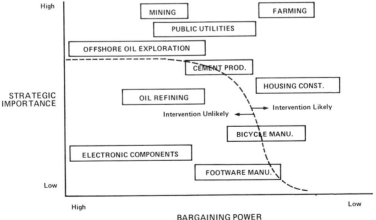

Industry Type

Several arguments can be put forward to say that intervention can be substantially explained by the type of activity in which the subsidiary is engaged. In other words, because a firm is a manufacturer of, say, containers or consumer goods, its intervention experiences are pre-ordained.

It is my view that this statement is generally incorrect. No matter what the main activity of the firm is, there is still substantial managerial scope to vary all of the determinants of bargaining power: complexity, foreign managers, exports and intra-MNE sourcing. That is not to argue that intra-MNE sourcing is more feasible in certain industries than in others, but there is still considerable scope to improve or reduce one's bargaining position.

In terms of the operational and managerial complexity of the subsidiary, I can think of very few business activities where there is a single manufacturing or managerial approach towards production. Product processes vary by labour intensity, size and complexity of machinery, type of technology used, amount of self-manufacture of components or external sourcing and in a myriad of other dimensions.

Chapter 7 will suggest a situation where even greater divergence of corporation behaviour in the same industry is possible: the successful management of those corporate variables which determine intervention. As in implementing any strategy, firms differ more often in the success of their implementation than in the differences among their strategies per se.

Empirical proof of this is found by examining the intervention experiences of industry groups. Here one finds considerable divergence. This divergence, although great, probably centres around different means (see Poynter, 1978). Firms in the natural resources sector seem to experience far greater intervention on average than any other industry type. Similarly, manufacturers of consumer goods experience more intervention than industrial goods manufacturers.

The important point for any observer, though, is that the amount of intervention variation *within* each industry-type exceeds the differences *between the means* of each type. Being a producer of manufactured industrial goods does not guarantee you less intervention than that felt by a firm involved in mining; experiences vary too much.

Factors without Influence over Intervention

Because the subject of government intervention has its own share of beliefs about causes and effects, it is worthwhile to elaborate briefly on those factors which experience and research have permanently relegated to mythology.

Spokesmen from developing and developed host countries and others have made extensive and frequent use of the United Nations and other private and multilateral forums to criticize MNE practices. (See United Nations, 1983). One could not blame MNE executives for thinking that the subjects of host countries' criticisms are ones to which they should direct their attention.

Prominent among the criticisms is the poor economic contribution of subsidiaries to the host nation. The author has examined five economic variables and has found no relationship whatsoever with the subsequent intervention experiences of the firms involved (Poynter, 1978, 1982). These economic performance indicators were calculated for each firm and included:

1. effect on the nation's balance of trade;
2. direct monetary contributions to the host nation (taxes, etc.);
3. profit repatriation rate;
4. parent company injections of external funds to subsidiary (foreign currency funding, debt, etc.);
5. personnel training (controlling for company size).

The most immediate conclusion arising from these results is that there is a large credibility gap between the rhetoric of host leaders on economic matters and their intervention behaviour. Even if it is assumed that governments do not have access to the range of information this author has, no one economic component plays an influential role. All of the variables have been found to be independent of intervention.

On the surface, the activities of the ever increasing number of economists and financial advisors working with the LDCs would tend to refute this finding. At the same time, however, there was no indication from government officials that such information was calculated for each company, although the poor economic performance of 'all our foreign companies' was mentioned inevitably when the subject was raised. Neither is it clear that the views of government economists normally affect senior civil servants and politicians. It would be premature to suggest that government leaders do not informally consider economic contribution, but the rhetorical preoccupation with this factor is not usually translated into action.

Conclusion

Two fundamental conclusions arise from an examination of the corporate determinants of intervention. The *first* is that a host government *does* discriminate among foreign companies when making the decision to intervene. Where across-the-board intervention policies exist, the discrimination normally takes the form of varying degrees of enforcement.

Second, this intervention is *not* a state of nature beyond the control of firms. Government behaviour in this regard can be partially explained in terms of particular corporate characteristics and policies. Most of these corporate attributes can be manipulated to reduce intervention.

Observations and research results show that the *bargaining power* model of government intervention is a good one. Four corporate characteristics determining the firm's bargaining power were found to be associated with the extent of intervention.

Two additional characteristics which partially defined the subsidiary's *political* exposure were found to have an association with intervention. Holding the firm's bargaining power constant, firms having a strategic importance in the host nation, and large firms were found to experience above-average intervention. It appears that small corporate size – and, therefore, a small number of employees – reduces the attractiveness of the firm to intervention-prone political party activists and trade unions.

Notes

1. Differences can persist even within this industry group. Production may utilize old, uncomplex machinery or new, highly technical machines with a small workforce. Similarly, a subsidiary may use marketing strategies formulated locally by subsidiary marketing executives, or it may use a slightly modified version of the home nation's marketing strategy. And it can use marketing executives from its home nation – expatriates – or domestic executives.

2. These projects used different indicators of the amount of intervention experienced. Fagre and Wells and Lecraw used the foreign equity percentage, Bradley used the expropriated – not expropriated dichotomy, while Poynter used a series of indicators which represented the amount of forced change a firm underwent due to intervention.

3. For further discussion of the role of these factors see Poynter 1978, 1982.

5 NATIONAL DETERMINANTS OF INTERVENTION

Why does Brazil intervene more than Indonesia, and Indonesia more than Kenya? Why do petrochemical firms in Mexico have to upgrade and expand in their protected market every three or four years to avoid intervention, while similar operations in Bolivia go unaltered for a decade or more? The answers seem to lie in two areas: the nation's bargaining power, and the international and domestic political circumstances.

In the previous chapter we reviewed those factors which determine the intervention risks of the MNE subsidiary. The most influential determinant, the subsidiary's bargaining power, deters intervention when domestic interventionists perceive it to be greater than their own bargaining power relative to the needs of that particular subsidiary.

In this chapter we shall consider the determinants of the host interventionist's bargaining power. This can help us understand why, for example, the Kenyan subsidiary of an MNE experiences little intervention while its duplicate in Nigeria has the opposite experience. As in the previous chapter, we shall also evaluate those factors affecting intervention which lie outside the bargaining power approach. Here, those factors are mostly political in nature.

One point of clarification first. I am concerned here with national levels of intervention and national discriminatory behaviour in implementing intervention. I am not concerned with predicting political risks caused by political instability, revolt and changes in regimes. These occur and can sometimes — but never always — result in intervention. As Hawkins, Mintz and Provissiero (1976), and Moran (1980) and others have suggested, most costly interventions occur during periods of relative stability. (As I shall argue near the end of this chapter, intervention is also rather independent of the amount of instability.) Fundamental indigenous upheaval is no longer the focus of attention for foreign direct investors intent on avoiding intervention.

National Determinants: Bargaining Power

Subsidiaries, like all other productive organizations, are dependent upon technology and skill, resources and a market for their output. Control over these elements determines the distribution of bargaining power and hence the costs and benefits of intervention. Multinational firms generally provide most of the technology (product, or managerial) to the subsidiary and a large part of the resources (capital, raw material, etc.). MNEs seldom control access to their market, however. For the purposes of this study of bargaining power, access to the market is considered to be controlled by the host government.

The amount of bargaining power in the hands of the interventionists and their government is determined by the amount and significance of their contribution to those three factors: technology, resources and market. Firms that are able to supply all or most of the first two and, in addition, find that the market controlled by the government is small, will have the greater amount of bargaining power. As the size of the local market grows, or as the ability of the host government to supply the other two factors increases, the bargaining power of the host nation increases and intervention rises.

The sources of bargaining power to be derived from the three key factors are worth describing in some detail. The factor for which the host nation is almost always at a bargaining disadvantage is access to technology. Multinationals exist because of their ability to generate and use managerial and product technology, and transfer it internally across frontiers and cultures. Loss of this key skill threatens the MNE's existence.

Technology

While lack of competitive technology is a casual and sometimes chronic condition of nations which are hosts to MNEs, changes in this area are most frequently responsible for intervention. As explained in Chapter 3, nations improve their technological skills over time and sometimes at quite a rapid pace. The improvement occurs mostly through internal skill generation. However, other possible ways are skill transfers through private and public means such as consultants, licensing, etc. Foreign investors in Brazil, India or Singapore can attest to the rapidity of the learning process in those nations.

Subsidiaries may find themselves in circumstances where the gap between the MNE's contribution to the subsidiary's needed technology and the capabilities of the local entrepreneurs and managers may have narrowed. Consequently, the improved bargaining position of the host nation is no longer reflected in the distribution of the benefits, for example, most go to the MNE, little to domestic parties. While the host nation was entirely dependent upon the MNE at the time of the original investment, local abilities have grown to the point where they can ably replace parts or all of the activities performed by the MNE.

To illustrate the point, a manufacturing subsidiary may find the abilities of local fabricators have risen to the point that the local businessmen will press the government to require greater local value-added. This will force the subsidiary to buy locally rather than import. This intervention is costly to the extent that local products are uncompetitive with imports.

When large numbers of the subsidiary's activities can be assumed by local businesses, intervention comes in the form of forced joint ventures and the like. Alternatively, pressure can be put on the subsidiary to expand its operations, while including local firms in its expansion. Government intervention in India often takes the latter approach. Brazil and other nations summarily legislate particular activities off-limits to MNEs.

Resources

The second factor determining the allocation of bargaining power is access to non-technological resources necessary for the subsidiary's success. These resources could include components for a manufacturing process, raw materials, concentrate for a chemical or food process, risk capital, political contacts, etc. Whether the MNE or the host nation holds the upper hand is to a large degree a function of the type of business activity involved. Mining companies, for example, go through a rather interesting bargaining power permutation as they establish a mine. Any discussion of technology or markets aside, mining companies find that their control over the capital necessary to find and develop a mine site provides the mining firm with the larger amount of bargaining power. Once built, however, another kind of resource assumes primacy, namely control over continued access to the natural resource. Control then swings back to the host nation. A brief examination of the intervention experiences of most international mining firms would corroborate this model with unilateral contract renegotiations occurring soon after production starts. A superb example is provided by Theodore H. Moran in his description of copper mining in Chile (1974).

Other resources could include access to inexpensive energy (oil in the Middle East, electricity in Ghana) normally in the hands of the host; access to risk capital which is often supplied by MNEs, not only in developing nations but if the risk level is high in developed ones as well; and access to productive labour at wages under the world market price, as in pre-1980 Singapore.

Market Access and Attractiveness

The third and final factor in any enterprise's success is access to a market. This factor only features when the size of the market is sufficient to be desirable to MNEs. In certain nations the size and wealth of the market can be sufficient to provide a large amount of bargaining power to interventionists, namely Nigeria.

In other nations, the size and wealth of the market for a particular product can provide so little profit to the MNE under normal conditions that control of it does not provide significant power to interventionists. There is, of course a continuum of market attractiveness on which combinations of nations and markets can be arraigned. Motor-cycles would have greater market attractiveness – and bargaining power to interventionists – than would electronic-component manufacture in Nigeria.

The high attractiveness of a local market also brings players other than domestic firms into the intervention equation. Large markets for particular products will attract the continuing attention of more than one MNE. So not only does the resident subsidiary have to deal with competition from domestic interventionists, but also from other MNEs. The astute host government will either utilize or cultivate such competition because it allows the government to increase its level of intervention (Moran, 1979; Fagre and Wells, 1982).

This inter-MNE competition was historically restricted to the selection of the first entrant into the host nation. MNEs traditionally would cease competition after the winner was selected. That tradition is under attack now from independents in the oil industry, new manufacturing MNEs from Asia and newly aggressive MNEs from Western Europe. This competition need not be for the right to establish another subsidiary. Often outside competition will offer to unbundle, suggesting joint ventures, licensing agreements and the like. This side-effect of competition increasingly provides the impetus for host-government intervention against the existing subsidiary.

While large market sizes are the main determinants of a host nation's bargaining position, as discussed in Chapter 4, MNEs can only acquire bargaining power in this area through exports to a protected or controlled market or, through intra-MNE sourcing. Both these sources of balancing the host's market-based bargaining power require the export market to be effectively beyond the reach of host interventionists. As mentioned earlier, the growth of bilateral trade, commodity markets and large multi-product trading houses reduces this source of bargaining power to the MNE.

To summarize the national determinants of bargaining power for each nation, we have a combination of natural attributes and ones that are more changeable, albeit slowly. For each particular product or subsidiary each nation has a level of bargaining power ordained by, first, the resources and capabilities important to that subsidiary and their relative cost in the host nation and, second, the attractiveness of its domestic market to the subsidiary and the degree of competition among MNEs that permits. These determinants of bargaining power change slowly over time.

Bargaining power changes more quickly in the supply of needed technology. Host-nation entrepreneurs, technicians and outside consultants acquire skills that reduce the technological lead and importance of the MNE. That is not to say that the parent MNE will not continue to gain technologically, only that the technology inherent in the operations of the subsidiary has come within the grasp of the domestic level of technology. The obvious, but not inexpensive, suggestion that the MNE increase the level of technology or skills required in its subsidiary will be discussed as we implement an intervention management strategy in Part 2 of this book.

National Determinants: Political

Intervention is a political act either in its formulation or enforcement. Politicians or civil servants must in some way pass judgement upon the desire of other domestic groups to intervene in order that the intervention has the force of law, or at least government support. Like all political policies then, the practice of intervention is affected by anything that alters the domestic political environment.

By reviewing intervention case studies, and after working with several host governments through periods of moderately heavy interventions, I contend that there are three environmental factors which determine the host nation's proclivity to intervene in a particular firm's operations:

1. bilateral and multilateral political relationships;
2. the political ideology of the ruling party and the civil service;
3. political system stability.

Bilateral and Multilateral Relations

Relationships between nations sometimes play a role in determining intervention. It is not difficult to see how intervention in a subsidiary whose *home* nation provides some desirable service to the *host* nation sometimes has a cost to the interventionist. Home nations can be providers of aid — especially desirable discretionary aid — lend money, provide military or economic support, or act as a supporter in multi-lateral organizations such as the World Bank, the United Nations, etc.

To the extent that host-nation politicians and civil servants hold this support desirable and difficult to replace, one would expect inter-vention in subsidiaries from the supporting nation to be reduced. This rather imposing and dramatic control over intervention has many limitations, however.

The power of this factor to affect intervention is limited by the degree to which the home nation's support is irreplaceable and by the power of the MNE to influence its home nation's foreign policy. Given the extent of competition among nations to replace each other as patrons, relatively few patrons want to jeopardize their relationship for fear that the supported nation may switch sides. This switching of alliances is not necessarily of the East-West type either. Within the Western world there is a competition for client states. So, for example, West Germany may have particular influence over some Arab states, the US over others, as may the French and the British. Because of this competition, then, Western nations which have established a supportive relationship with a particular developing country are hesitant to jeopardize the relationship for one MNE. Furthermore, after the ITT affair in Chile, the power of MNEs to affect their home nation's foreign policy appears to have been reduced. One should be careful not to assume that the US government ignores the interests of its MNEs totally, or that other home nations are as affected by international and domestic criticism of MNE-home government linkages as the US appears to be. Some European nations, in particular, have developed reputations as being strong supporters of their MNEs who, in turn, have strong voices in their own government.

While the role of government-to-government relationships in re-ducing intervention is difficult to document and, in practice, subject to the above limitations, intuitively it has great appeal. Given that intervention is affected by the costs and benefits of selecting one foreign firm over another, the thought that one firm's home nation provides significant foreign aid is bound to reduce the likelihood of intervention. A superficial examination of the intervention behaviour of Mexico and Brazil will illustrate the limits of such influence, however. The strong political economic and military relationships between those nations and the US did not apparently reduce the inclusion of US-owned subsidiaries in these countries' intervention activities. Here the significant costs to the US of utilizing its influence to reduce intervention were too great.

Ideology

The second element, political ideology, becomes important when one considers that the attitudes of the key decision-makers constitute a critical element in determining the formulation and selective application of the host government's intervention policy (Perlmutter, 1972). It has been suggested that these individual attitudes are influenced not only by the presence of local interest groups as discussed before, but also by their political ideology and historical circumstances.[1]

One becomes aware of the significance of political ideology if one considers the already tenuous nature of host-government decision-making concerning MNEs. As Ray Vernon saw it, '. . . the less-developed countries' view of foreign direct investment is not the outcome of a systematic toting up of pluses and minuses; it is much more an intuitive leap to a critical conclusion based on the prevailing interpretation of the history of foreign investment' (Vernon, 1966). LDCs are not a homogeneous group and, for the institutionally more-developed nations, decisions concerning MNEs are more 'systematic' than 'intuitive'. However, for the majority of LDCs Vernon's description — albeit over 15 years old — would still apply.

Decision-makers in LDCs, indeed most learned businessmen and academics, typically make equivocal statements about the value of MNEs' contributions. Because the social and economic cost-benefit analysis concerning most MNEs is usually seen to be only marginally positive or negative, one could propose that for many subsidiaries the political factor emerges as an important element of the host intervention policy, moving perceptions slightly to the left or right. (In addition, it follows that a significant proportion of the variance in the average level of intervention between countries can be explained on the basis of the prevailing host-nation ideology.) At the margin then, ideology plays a deterministic role.

Host nations which contain ruling politicians or civil servants noted for their leftist, socialist, or anti-capitalist stance (distinctions imposed by these groups, not the writer) will almost always tend to obtain greater rewards from intervening in subsidiaries which epitomize the ideological opposite. A review of the experiences of US-versus French-owned firms in India during the 1970s would illustrate the point.

While ideology does play a major role for certain subsidiaries, ideological differences seem oddly out of place in many explanations of intervention. The reason is that the ideological differences among developing countries seem to play less of a role in prescribing economic policies than they have in the past. More and more national policies for managing MNEs are noted for their similarities rather than their differences. A similar description could be applied to the political behaviour of MNEs, although this may have always been the case. Most MNEs, whether they are from the US, Mitterand's France or Schmidt's West Germany, appear politically to act quite similarly.

Political Stability

The final political factor influencing a host nation's intervention policy is political instability. As was discussed in Chapter 3, one has to distinguish here between intervention caused by revolution or instability per se, and intervention caused because the new decision-makers in place after a change in power will calculate the costs and benefits of intervention differently.

The role of political instability *per se* has, I believe, been over emphasized. As Hawkins, Mintz and Provissiero (1976), Robock (1971), and other observers constantly note, political instability does not necessarily lead to costly intervention. In addition, we do not appear to be very good at forecasting the occurrence of political instability. Accurate prediction is most difficult, if not impossible; attempts to predict or discriminate among nations regarding their likelihood for instability are characterized by high cost and a false sense of security based on the initial results and subsequent updates. An evaluation of Washington's totally inaccurate reading of pre-Khomeini Iran provides ample illustration of the state of the art.

While forecasting instability may be of little practical use, it may be worthwhile to consider any change in the nation's intervention behaviour that could take place because of a threatened or actual revolution or coup. There are a number of reasons why new governments intervene in the operations of foreign-owned firms. Ideology and other factors aside, taking action against foreigners tends to be beneficial to the political leaders. Accusing foreigners of misdeeds consolidates the population behind their new leaders and against those who are unquestioned 'enemies of the state'. So the greater the instability in a nation, the greater the benefits to be derived from intervention. While it is of little consolation to the unfortunate foreign firm suffering because of the instability, firms must differentiate this government behaviour from normal intervention.

Sometimes this kind of intervention goes to extremes, such as in Castro's Cuba, and then affects all foreign firms. In most cases, though, politicians discriminate and intervene in some but not all subsidiaries. There are a few reasons to assume that the basis of this discrimination is different from the intervention model presented in this book: a systematic analysis of the costs and benefits to be derived from each intervention, with the relative bargaining power of each firm a major determinant. When the driving force for the intervention is the con-solidation of political power, the only ingredient one should add is the political benefit to be derived from attacking prominent foreign firms with an eminently 'untrustworthy' nationality. Examples are US MNEs in most of the world, Hong Kong- or Chinese-owned firms in Indonesia, etc. But the political benefits from intervening in some firms are low. While almost all foreign attention was directed on the subsidiaries that had left Allende's Chile, subsidiaries of Bata Shoes and other MNEs still operated without experiencing costly intervention. Even in Khomeini's Iran, in a nation operating under great duress and little apparent economic rationality, several foreign firms still operate successfully.

The second and more prevalent manner in which political instability plays a role in determining intervention is in the different results reached by the new leaders as they calculate the costs and benefits of intervention. Whereas their predecessors may decide that expected costs outrun the benefits from a particular intervention, the new decision-makers − and their supporting civil servants and businessmen − may see a net positive benefit. Although the causal instability was not severe, Indira Ghandi's policy shift against MNEs in the mid-1970s is an example. The opposite, of course, is also true, as the early months of de la Madrid's term in Mexico illustrated.

The basis of the new leaders' different estimates of the costs and benefits of intervention seem to be consistent. In conversations with host-nation politicians and businessmen and the affected subsidiaries, the two sources of differing estimates are, first, the assessment of the subsidiary's technologically-based bargaining power and, second, the relative desirability of the home market to the subsidiary. Both processes are complex and prone to errors, such as India's in mid-1970. Brazil's late-1970's change appears to reflect an accurate re-estimation, however.

A more beneficial kind of political risk analysis to engage in, then, would be to try and predict intervention measurement changes in existing or future key policy-makers. This would not be any easier than predicting political instability, but the information would be continually useful during the more prevalent periods of stability and bargaining power-based intervention, and it may even be more accurate than instability forecasts.

Summary

Research has shown that the intervention behaviour of a nation towards a particular subsidiary is fundamentally determined by that nation's bargaining power with respect to the particular activity performed by the subsidiary, and by a collection of mostly political factors.

Nations (politicians, civil servants, entrepreneurs, businessmen, managers and technical staff) derive their bargaining power from their control over, and the significance of, each subsidiary's need for technology, resources and market access. The locus of control over the dominating factor determines the distribution of bargaining power and, hence, the level or frequency of intervention. This level of bargaining power is a function of the specific kind of business engaged in by the subsidiary, and the way it operates that business. Nigeria's bargaining power over a manufacturer of motor-cycles is high because of Nigeria's control over access to its large (population of 77 million), relatively wealthy, market for motor-cycles. Motor-cycles, however, can be made in several ways. A highly automated, efficient motor-cycle plant in Nigeria with imported components and some exports would have greater bargaining power than would an uncomplex, domestic market, plant.

The second set of determinants of a nation's intervention behaviour is mostly political in nature. Their specific importance in determining intervention appears to be declining as national economic policies appear to become more separated from political ideology.

Notes

1. For an example of how ideologies can produce diverse host perceptions of the MNE see A.B. Armstrong, *Toward a Systems Approach to Foreign Wealth Deprivation in the Developing Countries: The Tanzanian Case* (unpublished PhD dissertation, University of Washington, 1972) pp. 90 *et seq.*

6 CORPORATE BEHAVIOUR AND INTERVENTION

In any system of relationships, not only does hierarchy and differences in power influence the nature of the relationships, but so does the style or behaviour of the parties involved. In the relationship between subsidiaries and host-nation groups, the behaviour of the subsidiary, or more precisely its executives, seems to play a role in defining the views of influential domestic groups.

Broadly speaking, subsidiaries can become rather active in host-nation decision-making, and exert a consequential strong influence on domestic perceptions of the subsidiary, whether good or bad. Alternatively, the subsidiary can opt out, leaving it up to the government and domestic interventionists to formulate their own perceptions and policies.

For the activist subsidiary, the primary aspect of corporate behaviour is the way it affects domestic perceptions of the firm's bargaining power. While one can consider the absolute and objective estimates of the subsidiary's bargaining power to be determined by operational complexity, control over exports, intra-MNE sourcing, etc., intervention is really based on the subjective estimates or perceptions of domestic interventionists. To varying degrees, certain kinds of behaviour by companies can influence these perceptions. Because of the nature of this particular corporate activity, I refer to it as corporate political behaviour in order to differentiate it from other kinds of corporate activities.

Subsidiary executives are also involved in two other activities which have more direct effects. They collect intelligence about proposed intervention policies and the government's or sponsor's real expectations. In addition, subsidiaries can become involved in the intervention process so as to reduce its impact on the firm.

In this chapter, I will examine the various types of behaviour subsidiaries can engage in, both in developing and developed host nations. Particular corporate policies towards political involvement will also be examined. Research into the political behaviour of foreign firms has shown that even firms which do not have explicit political involvement seem to exhibit remarkable consistency in their political behaviour. Finally, the effect of these various policies on the subsidiary's intervention experience is outlined.

Corporate Behaviour: a Description

It would not be wildly inaccurate to separate subsidiaries into two distinct groups: those who actively participate in host-nation non-business activities, and those who opt out, playing no direct role in such activities. In four nations I examined in some detail, approximately 25 per cent of the subsidiaries studiously avoided any direct contact with the host government, or any other behaviour which would raise its profile (Poynter, 1978).

The maintenance of a low political profile dominates the thinking of this kind of subsidiary. Executives in these firms hardly ever initiate contact with domestic groups, including government, unless it is absolutely required for business purposes. If it becomes necessary, say a law affecting the subsidiary's operations is being considered, this kind of firm will try to use an intermediary of some sort before resorting to direct contact. Popular intermediaries are chambers of commerce, host nationals on the subsidiary's board of directors and the corporate lawyer.

What kinds of subsidiaries prefer to adopt this behaviour? Interestingly, the answer is that examples of all types of firms seem to behave this way. In an examination of over 100 subsidiaries, I did notice that these firms were generally managed by executives with comparatively little knowledge of domestic political affairs. Whether this caused the non-involvement, or resulted from it, is unknown. Executives who do not meet or negotiate with host nationals seldom have any need for anything but basic social-political data. (A few firms, we suspect, would never behave this way, because of the strategic significance of their operations. Those in the natural resource sector or in public utilities are classic examples.)

Should MNEs prefer this low-profile subsidiary behaviour, it may be interesting to examine the policy's other attributes. Talking with MNEs, it becomes clear that the low-profile policy fits well with an MNE strategy of high turnover of subsidiary general managers. MNEs — mostly US ones — which frequently send promising young executives to run subsidiaries for three years find that this behavioural policy matches the general manager's low level of political knowledge.

This low-profile strategy also is frequently appropriate in those MNEs where considerable emphasis is placed on the technological or functional expertise of the subsidiary's managers. Many, but not all, of these MNEs find that their organizational structure, promotional systems, reporting procedures and the like are not flexible enough to accommodate executives whose core skills are political rather than technical. Certain firms seem to have a limited tolerance for different kinds of executives, hence a technology-driven firm is more at home with a low political profile appropriate to its lack of politically-adept executives.

One must be careful not to assume that all subsidiaries with low-profile or non-involvement policies have politically-unaware or short-term general managers. For reasons discussed later in this chapter, many experienced, politically-competent general managers sometimes do decide that such a policy is appropriate and that its cost, the lack of input and the lack of awareness of proposed policies and government perceptions, is bearable by the subsidiary.

The majority of firms take a more activist stance in their general behaviour in the host nation. That is to not to say there is not considerable variation among firms. Some firms may attempt to do a considerable amount in this direction, or they may be incapable of doing much, but the decision to participate actively is present.

This participation takes on strong political overtones. Data on interest groups have to be collected, civil servants and politicians studied and relationships established, and local businessmen monitored. All of the activities result in some involvement, even a passive one, in domestic political processes. Subsidiaries, MNEs, host governments and assorted commentators and students of international business and political affairs have strong and often opposing views on such involvement.

Subsidiary managers speak of being involved in domestic politics. Host nationals sometimes use the terms meddling or interfering to describe the same activity. Whether or not this political activity is legitimate is, I think, a point better discussed elsewhere. Involvement per se in domestic politics cannot be wrong; what one does under the title of involvement is, of course, subject to review. The subsidiary, because of its wealth-generating role, has little control over its involvement in domestic politics. Any organization which is wealthy, frequently deals with political leaders and civil servants on business matters and is seen to represent an alien force, becomes, *de facto*, a political actor.

Subsidiaries which decide to play a participative role in understanding and managing their host-nation environment are not all equally prepared to pursue these activities. The better prepared firms have substantial knowledge about host politicians and other influential parties. This knowledge is not restricted to names and personality traits, but includes background material concerning their support group, social, economic, political and self-interests and their expectations. These kinds of subsidiaries need sufficient information so that when a problem arises, they know *whom* to see, *how* to arrange an appropriate meeting and *when* it should take place. These firms maintain a high political profile, are well known by influential host decision-makers and spend large amounts of executive time maintaining the links.

These politically-involved firms are also characterized by presidents or general managers with little turnover of position. The general managers are not transferred every three years or so and use the time in each host nation to become knowledgeable and establish relationships (not necessarily friendships) with influential people (see Poynter, 1978).

Not only are the influential aware of the subsidiary's activities, but, frequently through media campaigns and special projects, the general population is also influenced by the subsidiary. These firms are active in trade associations, government commissions and study groups, and will consider any kind of government or industry programme which will increase their exposure and knowledge.

The overall behaviour of these activist subsidiaries appears to embrace three kinds of activities:

1. influencing host-nation perceptions;
2. collecting intelligence about intervention sponsors and proposed intervention policies;
3. attempting to affect the intervention process and its implementation.

Subsidiary Behaviour and Host Perceptions

As explained in earlier chapters, the bargaining power of the subsidiary, relative to that of host interventionists, is the key determinant of intervention. Key characteristics such as operational and managerial complexity, exports, intra-firm sourcing and the proportion of expatriates in senior positions have been shown to determine the subsidiary's bargaining power. It is more accurate to say, however, that it is the interventionists' perception of the above four factors which prompts their intervention policy.

While the most effective way for subsidiaries to improve their perceived bargaining power is to increase or modify the above four key determinants, an additional method is to affect perceptions per se. Some firms attempted this by artificially increasing the perceived complexity of their operations through unnecessary numbers of expatriate engineers, excess security, etc. What appeared to be a far more successful and longer-lasting approach was to keep influential government officials and domestic business interests informed of the true bargaining power of the subsidiary. Executives kept these people informed of their parent's contribution to the subsidiary with regard to technology transfer and other resources, their plans for growth, the complexities of remaining competitive and expected changes in technology, etc. While exaggeration in the subsidiary's favour may occur from time to time, the overriding purpose is to ensure that host-nation perceptions accurately reflect the true allocation of bargaining power.

Intelligence Gathering

The second kind of activity engaged in by activist subsidiaries revolves around the collection of intelligence about intervention sponsors and proposed policies. Knowledge of the intervention sponsor puts the subsidiary in a better position to measure the likely extent and cause of the planned intervention. This makes it possible for the subsidiary to discuss the issue directly with the sponsor. This does not always diffuse the issue, of course, but allows the subsidiary to perhaps present its case, namely, that the costs of intervention would be greater than the benefits the interventionist hopes to realize.

This knowledge of the intervention sponsor also provides the opportunity to arrange some sort of intervention that would benefit the interventionist, but not at a high cost to the subsidiary. Examples of this strategy would be establishing the interventionist as a partner in another activity desired by the subsidiary. Alternatively, if the interventionist wants part of the domestic production quota, a product or component which will hurt the subsidiary least of all can be allocated to the domestic firm. This sometimes differs from the product the interventionist would most like to produce, but the new option is still appealing to the interventionist, as it results in less conflict and shorter negotiations.

The second benefit from this political assertiveness comes from knowing the extent to which the government intends to enforce the often global intervention policy. A large number of intervention policies *de jure* apply to all subsidiaries in the host nation. Sometimes these policies form part of political rhetoric and hence are meant for domestic political consumption only, and we are not intended to be seriously enforced. Other policies are meant for low bargaining power subsidiaries only.

That is not to say the host government would not like compliance by all firms, but that certain firms can detect an awareness in host policy-making circles that they are able to avoid compliance because of a perceived stronger bargaining position or other factors. As many subsidiaries in Nigeria found out, unnecessary compliance with Nigeria's myriad intervention policies brought with it no benefits of good citizenship, yet the cost of compliance was high, and it resulted in a considerable competitive disadvantage vis à vis those foreign firms which did not comply.

This knowledge of the true purpose and extent of planned intervention is probably the most significant product to be derived from intelligence gathering. As explained earlier, this importance is because most host governments discriminate among subsidiaries not only in the formulation of their intervention policy, but even more often in its application and enforcement.

Attempt to Reduce Intervention's Impact

The third and final kind of activity engaged in by MNE subsidiaries concerns attempts to reduce the impact of intervention. As described in Chapter 1, this activity mostly takes the form of attempts to escape from an already formulated intervention policy by putting external pressure on the host government. (This differs from 'using' one's bargaining power to avoid intervention as discussed in the preceding paragraphs.) In this case, subsidiaries use parent MNEs, home nations and other external sources of bargaining power. Because such power is external to the host government-MNE relationship, my impression has been that host governments react quite negatively to its use. While they may acquiesce to the pressure, it does tend to alter dramatically the subsidiary-host nation relationship and host perceptions of the subsidiary.

A description of the activist subsidiary would be misleading if it were to stop here. Much of what has been said suggests a positive outcome from such activist behaviour and that the low-profile, non-involved behavioural policy of subsidiaries would be second best.

Two drawbacks to the activist policy make the two different strategies more equal. First, becoming politically active does have its costs. The political profile of the subsidiary is raised, increasing the likelihood that the firm will be the subject of either an intervention policy or, as seen in many cases, the subsidiary will find that a hitherto unenforced intervention law becomes implemented. In addition, continued effective political involvement requires significant senior executive effort. There appears to be a high hurdle rate for involvement to be worthwhile: firms find they have an option of no involvement, or of spending considerable money and manpower collecting data and cultivating relationships. Similar to using exports as a deterrent to intervention, political involvement is only effective when engaged in to a significant degree.

Corporate Behaviour: Policy and Consistency

In evaluating the effects of these two opposing strategies, one quickly becomes aware of the strength of views held by MNE managers, views which are often diametrically opposed. Some executives call for active involvement in domestic affairs, learning about influential people, policy alternatives, etc. Others strongly hold to an apolitical policy of non-involvement, non-participation and hence restrict company activities to the traditional interpretation of business affairs.

Subsidiary managing directors and area managers frequently presented several examples to illustrate why their particular policy was preferred. Those which pursued a policy of general non-involvement presented examples exclusively based on their operations in countries where corruption was prevalent. A typical situation cited by a manager concerned his parent company's operation in India. Here, his company found that most federal and state 'recommendations' were never effectively enforced if the company simply ignored them. In addition, the company discovered that certain directives were issued by officials simply in an attempt to extort money from the companies. At the same time, this company, like several others interviewed, discovered that the initiation of contact with the host government — to discuss their recommendations for company action for example — frequently had the effect of stimulating increased demands from the officials rather than the 'improved understanding' the company was originally seeking.

These views are not only strongly held, but also result in a comprehensive corporate policy, even if only an implicit one, towards political and other domestic activities (see Poynter, 1978; 1982). I suspect that these policies are MNE-wide and govern the subsidiaries' behaviour in this regard.

In an attempt to evaluate the successes of both strategies, interviews with subsidiaries resulted in four measures which appear to reflect the political behaviour of firms. These are:

1. the proportion of significant host-nation contacts initiated by the firm;
2. the amount of time spent by executives and company lobbyists in discussions with the government (as compared to other firms in the host nation);
3. the amount of public relations;
4. the frequency of contact with non-ruling elites such as labour unions, opposition political groups, academics, etc.

Firms which ranked high on these measures over time were found to have a high level of knowledge about domestic politics, political process and intervention decision-making. It was also found that firms had similar scores on all four measures. Firms which have a relatively high number of contacts with the non-ruling elite also pursued an active public relations role, initiated most of the interaction with the government, and more frequently contacted the government, using both executives and domestic lobbyists. As one would predict, executives in these subsidiaries assessed themselves as having considerable knowledge of the local political situation. The opposite was also true.

Most firms see themselves as having a very activist political policy. However, when one compares their activities along the four dimensions discussed one finds − not surprisingly − that subsidiaries have divergent views of what constitutes political participation. Some, especially North American MNEs, believe that an awareness of appropriate rules and regulations, knowing the names and positions of several civil servants and the annual meeting with the Minister of Industry or whatever constitutes an activist stance. In reality, this has to be compared with, say, a French subsidiary, which knows that the Assistant Deputy Minister of Industry has a personal interest in a strong domestic manufacturing base in widgets.

For those firms considering an activist policy there are some direct implications for staffing policy. I contend that it is almost impossible to attain political knowledge sufficient to operate an activist policy when senior managers have short tenures, say two years, overseas. MNEs, identified mostly by their nationality, seem to differ significantly not only in their tenure policy but in their whole strategy towards international staffing. While this subject will be discussed in detail in Part 2 of this book, a few generalizations would be useful here.

European MNEs, for example, are often viewed as keeping their general managers overseas and in particular posts longer than do North American MNEs. It is generally accepted that this puts North American

MNEs at a disadvantage, at least on the political front, and in under-standing domestic policy-making.

This systematic disadvantage of mostly US MNEs appears to be coming to an end. Studies by New York recruiters Kenny, Kindler & Hunt, and Heidrick & Struggles found that over three times as many fast-track US executives want to work internationally in 1983 as did in 1973 (*Wall Street Journal*, 1983). The causes are uncertain, but the increasingly competitive situation US-owned subsidiaries face overseas, and the growth of foreign direct investment in the US are probably factors.

Company Political Behaviour and Intervention

Subsidiaries vary as greatly in their behaviour as they vary in size, complexity, external activities and bargaining power. It is not difficult to argue that such behaviour will affect the level of intervention experi-enced by the subsidiary. But because of the complexity and the positive and negative effects of each political behaviour strategy, it is not im-mediately clear which strategy is appropriate.

Using the four measures of political behaviour mentioned earlier in this chapter, I evaluated the intervention histories of approximately 130 subsidiaries in terms of their behavioural strategy (see Poynter, 1978; 1982). Adjusting for the effects of the subsidiary's bargaining power and other determining factors, the first conclusion one notes is that there are two sets of rules. One set of findings governs the smaller subsidiary, which is not involved in a strategic or a naturally high political profile activity; and the other governs its opposite, a firm which will be automatically visible either because of its size or strategic importance.

For small, low-profile firms, the cost of high executive involvement appears to be difficult to bear. Furthermore, their low profile provides some exclusion from intervention policies, if not in the formulation stage, at least in their implementation. For these firms the main defence from intervention comes from their small size. Consequently, they are correctly hesitant to do anything that would reduce any of the benefits of this near anonymity.

To these small firms, an increase in their participation and political involvement undoubtedly carries the benefits of a better understanding of host policies and provides the opportunity to influence policy out-comes. What appears to more than offset these advantages is the high cost — to the small firm — of acquiring and maintaining this high level of political activity, and the costs of acquiring a high political and economic profile. The latter brings with it undesired attention by government and domestic interventionists.

As subsidiaries grow with regard to their number of employees, their ability to avoid automatic inclusion in intervention policy-making and enforcement decreases. Once their inclusion becomes automatic, it appears that an assertive or activist policy of political involvement becomes more desirable, reducing the level of intervention experienced.

Large or high-profile firms which were neither actively involved, nor knowledgeable enough to initiate contacts with the host government, experienced more intervention than their more activist counterparts. Again, this finding holds even when one accounts for differences in bargaining power and other corporate determinants of intervention. In other words, after you have de facto become a political actor because of your significance or role, intervention can only be reduced ceteris paribus if the firm acquires sufficient knowledge, contacts and skills to play the role well.

Summary

Few subsidiaries of multinational enterprises can avoid becoming involved in the political as well as economic affairs of their host nation. For most it is not a matter of choice; their size, wealth and foreigness ordain their involvement.

What subsidiaries do under the title of involvement affects their level of intervention. While the main ingredients of the firm's bargaining power play the major role, it is the host nation's perception of the firm's bargaining power which is the final determinant. Each subsidiary can affect the interventionists' perceptions by playing an activist political role.

There are additional benefits from such an activist role. Subsidiaries can better understand the true nature of intervention policies, resulting in fewer situations of needless adherence to unintended policies. Intervention sponsors can also be identified, understood and beneficially negotiated with — sometimes.

This political activism is not without its costs. The ability to influence and be heard brings with it a high profile. Firms with high profile find themselves subject to the consideration and attention of other influential people and organizations. An additional cost is represented by the amount of senior executive time required to be politically involved successfully. These kind of executives are relatively scarce, and expensive.

Overall, however, such active involvement in one's political environment tends to pay off handsomely. Such firms experience significantly less intervention, on average, than do other uninvolved firms. There is an exception though. Subsidiaries involved in a non-strategic industry employing less than 75 or so employees are able to ignore successfully any significant interaction with host officials. Their low political profile provides them with almost automatic exclusion from all but the most comprehensive of intervention policies.

PART TWO: THE MANAGEMENT OF INTERVENTION

7 MANAGING INTERVENTION: THE SUBSIDIARY

Part 1 of this book provided a description of the causes and the nature of government intervention. Intervention, it has been argued, is not experienced equally by all, but varies from subsidiary to subsidiary. The causes of this variation are more likely to be found within each subsidiary rather than in the unique characteristics of each host nation. Each subsidiary has policies, strategies and characteristics which determine its absolute level of bargaining power. It is the level of bargaining power which appears to determine the extent of costly, forced, government intervention.

Part 2 of this book is concerned with the management of intervention. Most of the corporate policies and characteristics which determine intervention can be modified or changed by management action. In other words, actions can be taken which increase the subsidiary's bargaining power, thus reducing the likelihood of costly intervention.

Successful management requires MNE executives to be aware of their exposure to intervention risks. This section of the book will help executives construct a risk profile of each subsidiary, allowing them to estimate the likelihood of costly intervention. This allows MNEs to evaluate better both new investments, continuing operations and major capital expenditures.

The purpose of this section is to provide information so MNE executives can construct a survival plan. The plan outlines ways to reduce intervention, the costs of such a plan and the organizational and operational changes the firm would have to make to accommodate the survival plan.

The basis for the statements and conclusions of this part of the book differs from Part 1. A major segment of the concepts, analysis and conclusions of the first part involved the collection of a large amount of empirical data on subsidiaries and nations, preceded by interviews and discussions with all the interested parties. Because the idea of managing intervention is relatively new, most of the second part of this book came not from empirical investigation but from discussions with MNEs and subsidiaries who have — successfully or unsuccessfully — attempted to manage intervention. Some concepts were logically inferred from the findings of Part 1, and were subjected to critical evaluation and clarification by executives from 20 or so parent MNEs and approximately 50 of their subsidiaries. These executives also provided ideas, and opportunities for evaluating techniques and potential problems that could arise concerning the management of intervention.

As a result, Part 2 of this book is more exploratory and tentative than the first half. Some of the concepts and statements presented here have strong support, others are more speculative.

Part 2 divides the management of intervention into the two main structural levels of the MNE. In Chapter 7, the problem is discussed at the level of the subsidiary. Policies and actions subsidiaries can take to reduce intervention are discussed.

The proposed policies and actions vary when different countries and MNEs are considered. Therefore, Chapter 8 addresses the impact of host-country differences on intervention management. Subsidiaries from different kinds of MNEs also have to adopt different strategies for managing intervention. Multi-product MNEs like ITT present a different set of opportunities for managing intervention than does a single-product MNE like Coca-Cola and some of the MNEs involved in the food business. The last section of Chapter 8 examines this problem from the perspective of five different types of MNEs. Finally, Chapter 8 reviews the alternatives facing strategically important MNEs which traditionally experience high levels of intervention.

In Chapter 9 we move to the level of the MNE parent with the problem of managing intervention for a number of subsidiaries. Many of the subsidiaries' intervention-reducing policies affect the worldwide operations of the MNE. Consequently, the intervention policies of individual subsidiaries cannot be isolated from the others, as they are by their very nature interrelated. Hence intervention policy must to a large extent be centralized and highly co-ordinated. Chapter 9 illustrates this implementation aspect in detail.

Chapter 10 provides a summary of the book. Profiles of high- and low-intervention MNEs are provided and some of the major questions yet to be solved are discussed.

The Decision to Intervene

Part 1 of this book has argued that intervention primarily takes place against those subsidiaries where the intervention sponsors expect to realize a net gain. Research has shown that the main economic criterion used by interventionists as they scan the set of available subsidiaries is the significance of the MNE owner to the continued success of the subsidiary. From the interventionist's perspective, this significance automatically defines their ability to operate the subsidiary successfully without the co-operation of the MNE. This principle operates in both developing and developed nations, although the level of sophistication can be dramatically different.

The relative bargaining power of MNE and interventionists determines the amount of intervention in two ways. Prior to attempting intervention, the interventionist's perception of the power of the MNE will influence the interventionist's behaviour, with *ab initio* perceptions of high MNE bargaining power reducing or stopping intervention. Alternatively, aspiring interventionists either with, or represented by, their government, will start bargaining or negotiating with the MNE. During this negotiating process the relative bargaining power of both parties becomes more evident to each; positions are taken on the basis of the distribution of bargaining power, and feasible objectives are set. The outcome of this negotiating process can be called the intervention outcome.

One of the best means of evaluating the net gain to be derived by the interventionist is to measure the relative bargaining power of the foreign investor against the bargaining power available to the interventionists. The MNE's bargaining power is based on the key resources the MNE can supply, relative to their availability either in the host nation, or from other sources available to the host nation. As explained in Chapter 4 these key resources vary among firms, but generally control over and access to the following are present:

1. product and process technology;
2. managerial skills;
3. raw material, components and other manufacturing inputs;
4. export markets;
5. domestic markets.

Two characteristics of each of these resources define their role in determining the distribution of bargaining power: the relative importance of each factor to the subsidiary's success; and the relative control each party (MNE and interventionist) has over each factor or, in other words, their respective ability to replace the other's contribution or control.

Relative Importance

Each business activity places unequal emphasis on each of the five resources listed above. A subsidiary of the US-MNE 'Crown Cork and Seal Inc.' manufacturing aerosol cans, selling and maintaining bottling machinery in local plants as well as manufacturing bottle caps, relies primarily on access to, and knowledge of, process and product technology. While significant to Crown Cork, managerial skills, component supply and access to export markets are not of great importance to the success of the subsidiary. A subsidiary of 'Bata Shoe Limited', for example, will find that managerial skills rather than product technology are pre-eminent. Access to the domestic market is important because of the lack of export market in both cases. The significance of the domestic market is determined by the size and wealth of the market, with Nigeria's market being more significant than Sudan's for example.

Relative Control

The second characteristic determining the importance of the five resources above is the relative control each party has over each resource, and its ability to replace the other's role. We have discussed several times in this book how domestic interventionists such as businessmen and their support groups (including foreign consultants) can acquire product and process technology and learn managerial skills. Cases exist where MNEs can exclusively control raw materials or components, or there can be a free market in those inputs, or, as in the case of natural resource operations, the raw material can be under the control of the host. Export markets are usually under the control of the MNE, while domestic markets are usually controlled by the host nation. However, MNE control over export markets is being reduced by the growth of international trading firms.

The Intervention Equation

Using the five resources noted above, one can express the intervention equation algebraically as follows:

$$BP = (TECH \times W1) + (MGMT \times W2) + (INPUTS \times W3) \\ + (EXPORTS \times W4) + (MARKET \times W5)$$

BP represents the bargaining power of the party in question.

The variables TECH, MGMT, INPUTS, EXPORTS and MARKET

represent absolute measures of each party's ability to perform that role or supply that resource to the subsidiary over the next planning period. The weights W1 through W5 represent the relative importance of each of those five factors to the future success of the subsidiary in question. (This equation will be discussed and used later in this chapter.)

The bargaining power of the MNE and the local interventionist is computed for the subsidiary in question and, as has been shown in previous chapters, when $BP_{host} \geqslant BP_{MNE}$ intervention generally occurs. Some observers will argue that intervention will occur before there is an equality in BP. In other words, intervention may occur even before the host's domestic level of technology or access to export markets are equal to that of the MNE parent. After this happens, the subsidiary will make less profits and produce fewer overall economic benefits than before intervention. But other, non-economic, benefits in the social and political spheres offset these costs.

Figure 7.1: Relative Bargaining Power over Time

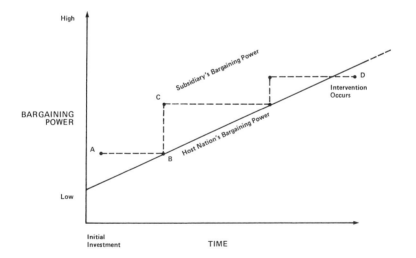

Figure 7.1 conceptualizes the basis of the subsidiary's intervention management problem. Upon entry into the host nation, the subsidiary's bargaining position is high (A). The investing firm's knowledge of the technology and management techniques necessary to operate successfully

is generally higher than the capabilities resident in the host country. Over time, however, this gap decreases. Host nationals learn either directly from the subsidiary, or through other means, such as other MNE subsidiaries, training, overseas education, etc. Consequently, the relative need for MNE involvement to ensure continued success of the subsidiary is reduced. In other words, the relative bargaining power of the MNE dissipates over time.

In the next section of this chapter we shall discuss how a subsidiary can find its position on Figure 7.1 and what actions it can take before point 'B' ($BP_{host} = BP_{MNE}$) is reached in order to improve its bargaining position to point 'C'.

Operationalizing the Intervention Model

Basic to any management of costly intervention is the determination of a subsidiary's bargaining position vis à vis any potential domestic interventionist's. One's position determines the probability of intervention, or some estimate of the time remaining before intervention occurs.

Accurate positioning on Figure 7.1 is necessary in order to avoid some of the high costs of increasing one's bargaining power too early or too late — after intervention occurred or after the generally irreversible decision to intervene has been made. As noted earlier, the improvement in a subsidiary's bargaining power often calls for an increased capital investment in the host country in advance of the MNE's original preferences. Additionally, because bargaining power is a dynamic concept, the bargaining advantage of, say, a technological upgrade begins to decrease the moment it is made. The decrease occurs because the skills inherent in the new technology are learned by host nationals, or are dissipated. To the MNE, therefore, *delaying* an upgrade as long as possible will prolong the bargaining power benefits.

Both these capital investment and skill-dissipation factors call for judicious and accurate timing of the bargaining power increase. Theoretically, the increase should occur just before local entrepreneurs or government officials notice the subsidiary's 'weakened' position (point 'B' in Figure 7.1).

To determine each subsidiary's position, we return to the bargaining power equation introduced earlier:

$$BP = (TECH \times W1) + (MGMT \times W2) + (INPUTS \times W3)$$
$$+ (EXPORTS \times W4) + (MARKET \times W5)$$

The calculation of this equation has to be, of course, dependent on considerable subjective input. One is attempting to measure things for which no objective measures have been developed and indeed may not even exist. The calculation, therefore, will be subject to some error.

To evaluate the seriousness of the measurement error one has to consider the precision of the activity the equation attempts to model. The activity is the decision of various groups in a country to agree on an intervention. Their decision, a highly subjective one, is based on the five factors in the equation. Hence, perceptional differences between the host-nation groups and the MNE executive determine the error. All of which makes this a rather rough calculation. Consequently, detailed or highly refined measures are out of place here.

The mathematical calculation of the equation's values provides few difficulties. In discussion with some of those executives who supplied the estimate for the intervention formula, it was found that five- or seven-point scales were appropriate. A higher level of discrimination would be misleading. In addition, for both MNE and domestic interventionists the relative importance or weights placed on each factor should be the same, because they refer to the subsidiary or business activity in question. Operationally defining the weights in percentages seems to be the most practical approach.

Factor Weights

An example will illustrate the approach. Table 7.1 shows the calculations of the factor weights for six firms. These weights represent the relative importance of each of the five factors to the future success of the subsidiary.

Table 7.1: Calculating Bargaining Power: Factor Weights

Subsidiary		Weights (%)[a]					
	TECH	MGMT	INPUT	EXPORT	MARKET		
Firm A : Shoes/Sudan	20	40	20	0	20	=	100
Firm B : Shoes/Nigeria	10	30	0	0	60	=	100
Firm C : Radios/Indonesia	20	10	30	35	5	=	100
Firm D : Lathes/Brazil	30	10	15	5	40	=	100
Firm E : Petrochemicals/ South Korea	40	10	0	15	35	=	100

Note: a. Rounded to nearest 5 per cent.

The subsidiaries and their parents are as follows:

Firm A: Shoe manufacturer; 150 employees; no exports; imports 5 per cent of 'cost of goods sold' (COGS) consisting of vinyl and other easily sourced goods.

Firm B: As Firm A but located in Nigeria; 500 employees.

Firm C: Radio manufacturer, consumer type; exports 80 per cent production, of which half is semi-completed, destined for an associated firm; 600 employees; imports 30 per cent of COGS, consisting of components and partially finished radios from affiliated firms.

Firm D: Machine lathe manufacturer, ranging from locally-produced small-bar manual types to large-bar automatic lathes imported and assembled; 15 per cent exports; 400 employees; 10 per cent of COGS imports, consisting of components and the more complex lathes from parent.

Firm E: Downstream, specialized petrochemical plant producing 15 different products; 180 employees; exports 30 per cent of sales; imports 65 per cent of COGS (petroleum foodstock).

Various techniques can be developed to provide these weights. For all but the domestic market factor, some firms find that the allocation of the general manager's time provides a good starting point for estimating the weights to use. Over the long term, senior executives usually concentrate on those areas of their business which are a key to their success. One can then adjust the time distribution to account for well organized and smoothly operating tasks, which nevertheless are a key to the business.

Using the parent MNE's proprietary chemical formulations or well-protected patents would be examples where adjustments are necessary. In the case of the domestic market's importance, several people criticize using executive time as an indicator of its importance because it increases with the amount of competition. However, increased competition usually suggests a large market, hence it is a good reflector of factor importance.

The weights change over time, too. A technological breakthrough in the lathe manufacture will increase the emphasis on technology.

Similarly, changes in the product mix offered by a subsidiary may change the overall emphasis from technology to management skills or to acquiring important manufacturing components.

Access and Control Variables

Determining the access and control values of the five factors is the more difficult of the two main tasks involved. The objective is to measure each party's access to, and control over, the specific resource. Some MNEs are the sole suppliers of the technology needed by the subsidiary, while in other cases that resource is available locally. Similar situations exist in the case of the other needed resources. For example, the domestic market is almost always under the control of the host government. But this may not be so when the foreign firm has little competition – foreign of domestic – while the subsidiary is operating, or little likelihood that other MNEs would push to replace the subsidiary should it cease operating. In those circumstances MNE access and control over the host market is not negligible. The task is essentially one of understanding and evaluating the subsidiary's domestic environment. While the approach mentioned here involves the separate estimate of both the MNE's and host's access and control scores, in practice one is estimating the gap or the difference between the MNE and the host. In order to measure this important gap, subsidiary management has to evaluate its own level of technical, managerial and other contributions to the subsidiary's success, and then compare this level to the availability of these skills in the host country.

While appearing relatively simple, this evaluation requires considerable information and insight. In practice, this involves monitoring the activities, growth and capabilities of existing or potential interventionists (i.e. businessmen, politicians, suppliers, etc.). To go back to the earlier illustration of the electro-mechanical firm, they will have to monitor the abilities of domestic manufacturers of the subsidiary's product or any of its imported components. When domestic firms can provide the same skills as the foreign firm (i.e. they are efficient enough to manufacture at similar costs), experience shows that intervention occurs. This intervention will be directed either specifically at the subsidiary (e.g. forced joint venture, licensing agreement, forced sourcing), or the domestic firm will establish a competing line where, in most cases, discriminatory government practices will force out the foreign firm.

In practice, the calculation of the gap between the MNE's and host's level of bargaining power expedites the whole process. The better approach seems to be to take the MNE's perspective and calculate its bargaining power compared to the host using a five- or seven-point comparison scale. The following is an example measuring the MNE's access and control over the technology necessary to keep the subsidiary successful:

Access to and Control over Technology

none	much less	slightly less	same	slightly more	much more	complete
0	1	2	3	4	5	6

A score of 5 means that the MNE has 'much more' access and control over the required technology than any other party or group in the host nation.

To illustrate the evaluation mechanics, a MNE manufacturer of radios located in Indonesia would, say, have a score of 3 (the default, base score) while any potential interventionist would probably score '0' (access to and control over radio technology: none). A lathe manufacturer in Brazil may find that potential interventionists may score 2 or even 3 and 4 on the management skill dimension.

Referring back to the bargaining power equation and using the seven-point comparison scale above, the MNE must have a weighted score higher than 3 (same access and control over the key resources necessary to make the subsidiary successful). An outcome less than 3 shows that the host nation has greater bargaining power than the MNE.

Table 7.2 provides the scores for the five subsidiaries introduced in Table 7.1. Table 7.3 brings both together to provide the overall BP scores for each subsidiary. It is clear from the latter table that two subsidiaries, the shoe manufacturer in Nigeria and the lathe manufacturer in Brazil, are likely to experience intervention. The petrochemical

Table 7.2: Calculating Bargaining Power: Factor Control

Subsidiary[a]		MNE's Access and Control[b]				
		TECH	MGMT	INPUT	EXPORTS	MARKET
Firm A:	Shoes/Sudan	5	6	4	5	2
Firm B:	Shoes/Nigeria	4	5	3	4	0
Firm C:	Radios/Indonesia	5	4	4	6	0
Firm D:	Lathes/Brazil	4	3	4	4	0
Firm E:	Petrochemicals/					
	South Korea	5	3	3	4	1

Notes: a. The subsidiaries and their parent MNEs are described on p. 90.
　　　 b. A seven point 0–6 comparison of the MNE's access to and control over each of the five factors or resources compared to the host nation. See text for a description of the comparison scale.

Table 7.3: Calculating Bargaining Power: Overall

Subsidiary[a]	Factor Values = MNE Control x Factor Weight[b]					
	TECH x W1	+ MGMT x W2	+ INPUT x W3	+ EXPORTS x W4	+ MARKET x W5 =	BP
Firm A: Shoes/Sudan	5 x .20	6 x .40	4 x .20	5 x .0	2 x .20 =	4.6
Firm B: Shoes/Nigeria	4 x .10	5 x .30	3 x .0	4 x .0	0 x .60 =	1.9[c]
Firm C: Radios/Indonesia	5 x .20	4 x .10	4 x .30	6 x .35	0 x .05 =	4.7
Firm D: Lathes/Brazil	4 x .30	3 x .10	4 x .15	4 x .05	0 x .40 =	2.3[c]
Firm E: Petrochemicals/ South Korea	5 x .40	3 x .10	3 x .0	4 x .15	1 x .35 =	2.25

Notes: a. See p. 90 for details.

b. Based on the bargaining power equation:

$$BP = (TECH \times W1) + (MGMT \times W2) + (INPUT \times W3) + (EXPORTS \times W4) + (MARKET \times W5)$$

c. BP results which indicate that the overall bargaining power of the MNE is less tnan that of the host nation, hence these firms are likely candidates for intervention.

producer while in a stronger position, is getting close to a situation where South Korea has an equally strong position.

What often comes as a shock to MNEs is the increasing number of alternative sources of needed components and access to export markets. Basing ones bargaining power on continued exclusive control over specific input requirements of protected export markets often turns out to be more short lived than even the most pessimistic MNE expectations.

Probably one of the more controlled industries in this regard is the bauxite and aluminium industry. The mining of bauxite, the raw material for aluminium production, is carried out by vertically-integrated firms such as Alcan, Reynolds, Alcoa etc. The main and almost exclusive use of bauxite is in the production of alumina and then aluminium ingots. These in turn are transferred to fabricating subsidiaries of the aluminium firm.

For good production and obvious intervention-reducing reasons, these three operations are usually performed in three different nations. Having almost complete control over both input and output provides these subsidiaries with a very high level of bargaining power. This is reflected in the relatively low levels of costly intervention experienced by the majority of aluminium MNEs, in spite of the high political profiles appropriate to their involvement in natural resources.

As Guyana's takeover of Alcan's bauxite operation shows, however, such protection is not always permanent. Observers suggest that Guyana's intervention was due to its belief that it could find alternative buyers for its bauxite in the Eastern bloc.

In addition, the resources that have to be devoted to this intelligence collection activity are not small. Middle-level executives who perform this function must be capable of objectively evaluating their own subsidiary's access to and control over the five key factors, and then evaluating the performance of the potential interventionists.

While the evaluation mechanics are relatively simple, the acquisition of the necessary intelligence is not. Potentially interventionists must be identified through close and informal relationships with domestic private businessmen and parastatal managers. Their competences, weaknesses and opportunities need to be monitored and kept up to date.

The Bargaining Power Upgrade

After the calculation of the relative bargaining power of the foreign firm and the feasible set of interventionists, it is now time to consider what actions should occur when the inevitable — for most subsidiaries — takes place: the gap between the MNE and the host nation decreases to the point where intervention is likely.

Conceptually, the ideal time to upgrade or increase one's bargaining power is just before the host nation's bargaining power is equal to that of the firm's (point 'B' in Figure 7.1). At this point the host-nation government or interest groups begin to believe that they can replace the MNE involvement with domestic technology/management/sourcing/etc. without too great a loss. By this time, MNE threats to withdraw services or skills hoping to prevent intervention are less of a deterrent to domestic entrepreneurs and others intent on obtaining part of the economic 'pie' created by the subsidiary.

A bargaining power upgrade at point 'B' would include any item which would improve a firm's bargaining position. For example, an additional product line, a more sophisticated process technology, new sourcing methods, etc., in other words, any activity which cannot easily be replicated by domestic skills. To illustrate this point further, for a subsidiary which has been importing electronic components for assembly into a mature electro-mechanical device, a bargaining power upgrade could involve the domestic manufacture of the more sophisticated electronic components not easily available in the host country. This could raise the subsidiary's position to point 'C'. Failure to upgrade one's bargaining position will eventually result in the subsidiary experiencing some form of costly intervention such as a forced joint venture, forced local-sourcing of components, etc. (point 'D').

Referring back to the five key factors determining the sources and distribution of bargaining power, an upgrading of bargaining power would be any corporate activity that would increase the MNE's position relative to the host nation's. The list in Figure 7.4, while not at all exclusive, illustrates a set of possible actions.

Table 7.4: MNE Actions Increasing Bargaining Power

---

1. Introducing a new and more complex/efficient process technology (material, machines, etc.)
2. Introducing new products or services; or better versions of existing product using existing technologies and management skills
3. Significantly improving exports, especially in cases where export markets are not easily developed or maintained
4. Increasing amount of intra-MNE sourcing either at input or output side

---

Implementation Issues

The financial and policy implications of these activities vary in significance, but are never minor. The management of intervention consists not only of estimating one's bargaining power vis à vis interventionists, but also of managing the implementation aspects of any activity designed to increase one's bargaining power.

Considering first the top two sets of activities in Table 7.4 (new process technologies, new products and new applications of existing technology and skills), the financial implications are somewhat obvious. Capital expenditures are required for new peoducts, machinery and for new manufacturing processes. Given that the products or processes are new, funds are required for training, personnel transfers and initial operating losses on the new line.

Transferring suitable product and process technology and managerial skills for the product or process upgrade can tax the most capable subsidiary. One characteristic of international business in the 1980s aggravates the problem: an increasing number of products and processes are being introduced around the world at a more rapid pace than in the sixties and seventies. Product lifecycle descriptions of products slowly moving overseas as they mature in their home market now appear to apply in few situations.

As a consequence of the speed of international propagation, new product or process innovations arrive at the overseas subsidiary with appropriate management policies not yet perfected. One of the historical benefits of being the recipient of a mature product or manufacturing process is that all the bugs would have been worked out and uncertainties reduced. Appropriate product characteristics, size, price, marketing strategies, sales policies and all the problems associated with new processes from preventive maintenance to production rates would have all been refined. On the other hand, we now find that relatively new products and processes contain much uncertainty.

This uncertainty makes the implementation of product and process upgrades more difficult. Introducing a mature product into a subsidiary only requires sufficient technical and managerial skill to adapt the transferred item to the new market. When that new product upgrade contains several uncertainties about appropriate management policies, the subsidiary requires even more refined technical and managerial skills to solve these more fundamental business problems.

The upgrade now requires not only adaptive management skills, but the ability to innovate and generate fundamental solutions to product characteristics, production and marketing. In other words, the subsidiary must now create a complete product strategy.

Some subsidiaries experience considerable problems in creating or obtaining their new technical and managerial skills. Subsidiaries located in the fast growing countries such as Brazil, Mexico, Nigeria, Singapore and South Korea have particularly difficult problems. Here, firms have had to upgrade products and processes rapidly. Within a few years subsidiaries have had to change from mature product firms operating in a protected market, to firms using the latest products and processes and competing, in some cases, in an open market at world prices.

Such a drastic change of subsidiary strategy does not come easily. The retraining of executives experienced in operating in low-efficiency, protected economies is slow and expensive. Often the only viable alternative is to bring in new executives, especially at the presidential or managing director level, in order to successfully implement the new strategy.

When the managerial skill level is high in the subsidiary, but is no longer fully utilized in the running of the business because the product line is established, another option for increasing bargaining power appears. This excess or surplus skill can be used on another problem outside the subsidiary's normal course of business. The cases of Union Carbide and British American Tobacco taking on failing fishing, clothing and lumbering operations in India illustrate the flexibility of this particular response. In return for this action, those MNEs negotiated and achieved relatively little intervention during a period when multinationals were having quite a difficult time in India. Others who have attempted this kind of strategy without a strong managerial team found the costs to be rather high.

The third option mentioned in Table 7.4 calls for increases in exports and especially exports not easily replicated by others. When exports meet the qualification 'not easily replicated by others' they are guaranteed to provide a significant bargaining advantage. Significant exports to markets where other domestic firms or helpful trading companies can duplicate the export effort appear to provide only short-term bargaining advantages.

According to most MNEs, however, the economics of exporting from subsidiaries in the majority of developing host nations are not good. A majority of manufacturing operations are below world scale and are protected. These subsidiaries can seldom export profitably into the world market. Exceptions are, of course, those subsidiaries which have expanded production facilities to be world competitive or which were established originally with export competitiveness in mind. In addition, subsidiaries in nations where raw material or other inputs such as electricity or labour are significantly below world prices also can take advantage of this option.

The final option of increasing intra-MNE sourcing or trade also has a great effect on the MNE. Efficient world-scale plants are required, along with a substantial degree of integration among the subsidiaries. Substantial intra-MNE trade in components and finished products is only feasible when prices and product performance are comparable with that of one's competitors. In the typical protected subsidiary producing components and end products above world prices, this option is costly. On the other hand, this option is very attractive for the subsidiary whose production facilities were improved or originally constructed to produce at close to world prices. In addition to requiring sufficient production facilities, all other domestic production inputs − plus management − also have to be sufficiently close to world prices, in order to be competitive.

This chronic problem of high-priced domestically-sourced inputs does not automatically preclude subsidiaries from improving their facilities so as to increase intra-MNE trade. Depending on the product, locally-sourced inputs such as steel or plastics may constitute a small proportion of the total cost and hence have little impact on final product costs.

In practice, the last option calls for greater concentration of production. Instead of manufacturing a component or product in, say, both India and Pakistan, the product would be manufactured in India − at a lower cost because of scale improvements − and shipped to the other. To balance the trade account and reduce government displeasure − and improve the availability of foreign exchange − the importing subsidiary, Pakistan, would reciprocate with another product, exporting it to India. The net result is two subsidiaries with improved bargaining prices and lower costs as well, because of the savings from larger-scale production. Of course, the cost savings and financial feasibility of the option is highly dependent on product characteristics such as scale economies, transportation costs and host-government policies towards importing from other developing countries.

These problems of inter-LDC trade, as in the case of the above two countries, are unfortunately large. There is still a large number of developing nations which, for egotistical, political and reasons of perceived quality differences, will insist on importing from, say, West Germany rather than their neighbour. Exacerbating this tendency is the fact that transport costs often bear little dependence on distance and depend more on the amount of competition. Transport rates among developing countries are frequently higher than developed-to-developing-country rates for similar distances.

There is, of course, no reason why one trading subsidiary cannot be in, say, France, and the other in the Ivory Coast or Nigeria. As a matter of fact, those MNEs with significant intra-MNE trade such as IBM and Black & Decker have significant north-south trade routes.

One of the reasons for some optimism concerning the sourcing option is that for very different reasons it is being pursued by various host nations. Canada, for example, would like many foreign subsidiaries there to specialize in few products, supplying them to the rest of the MNE. Canada pursues this so-called world product mandate policy because of its need for strategic managerial skills and the research and development activities such product specialization brings to Canada. (For details on this policy see Crookell, 1983, and Poynter and Rugman, 1982.)

Whenever there is such an increase in intra-firm trade or sourcing, there is a commensurate need for greater integration of decision-making. Not only do shipping schedules have to be agreed upon, but product standards, transfer costs, supply priorities, product improvements, market feedback and capital budgeting procedures have to be agreed upon and a procedure in place for problem-solving and modification to agreed-on procedure. Subsidiaries lose some of their autonomy as a result. This aspect of this option will be discussed in Chapter 9 when MNE-wide management of intervention is considered.

The Bargaining Power Upgrade: Reducing its Cost

All bargaining power upgrades are costly. New machinery, people, sources and markets have to be acquired, and a whole new set of problems have to be understood and solved. The cost is justified in terms of the direct reduction of intervention that the upgrade brings with it.

Certain upgrades cost so much, however, that their justification is not clear. Two clear examples are provided by the exporting and intra-MNE sourcing strategies. In many cases the costs of production are not competitive with the alternative locations and, hence, production has to be subsidized. Clearly, protecting a loss-making subsidiary from intervention is not worthwhile.

However, those two strategies provide such large increases in bargaining power that opportunities for creating offsetting profits are available. Other products or operations such as the importation and sale of the mature product, with a high profit margin can also be introduced. Their low bargaining power can be offset by the high power available from the export or sourcing strategy. Viewed in this manner the lower intervention risk — but often lower profits — offered by the two defence strategies allows the subsidiary to engage in normally unacceptable but profitable activities to provide an acceptable overall level of profits.

Additional means of reducing the costs of such powerful, but expensive, strategies is available from an unlikely source: the host government. Increasingly host governments are offering export and other incentives to subsidiaries as well as to domestically-owned firms. Host-government capital and operating subsidies, export support and similar activities can go a long way towards the costs of export and world product mandate strategies.

Summary

Intervention risks, like marketing and financial ones, can be substantially managed. They can be managed because, in all three cases, much of the risk can be influenced by actions taken by the organization in question. Subsidiaries can take actions which increase their perceived bargaining power. Policies or strategies can be put into place which ensure the timely and effective use of these intervention-reducing actions.

The management of intervention consists of three key actions. The first is the calculation of the subsidiary's bargaining power relative to the host's at a point in time. This calculation requires local intelligence, an objective viewpoint and a recognition that the concept of bargaining power is a dynamic one.

Deciding when and how to upgrade one's bargaining power is the second managerial action. Because such upgrades tend to dissipate as soon as they are made, judicious timing and appropriate selection is a key factor.

Finally, what may be the most difficult process is the successful implementation of the bargaining power upgrade. This takes place in a competitive world characterized by short product lifecycles and the rapid international transfer of complex technology, much of which still contains process, product and marketing uncertainties.

8 MANAGING INTERVENTION IN DIFFERENT NATIONS AND FIRMS

The preferred corporate policies for increasing bargaining power vary according to specific national and corporate characteristics. Preferred policies vary due to different national skills and the level of development. Similarly, multi-product MNEs have a different set of opportunities for reducing intervention than single-product MNEs. The purpose of this chapter is to discuss the impact of host-country differences and the various types of MNEs on the management of intervention.

Intervention Management in Different Nations

The multinational enterprise that manages intervention in several nations will find that the problem varies country by country. The main source of the variation is the difference in bargaining power of each host nation. Countries improve their technological and managerial skills through internal skill generation, and skill transfers from developed nations through private and public means. Market attractiveness, another source of variation, varies considerably among nations, a function of size and wealth.[1]

Variations in Bargaining Power

While empirical proof is lacking, one could suggest that for many reasons, individual nations are at different positions on the bargaining power ladder. Figure 8.1 indicates the overall bargaining power of several host nations based on the availability of technical and managerial resources, and the attractiveness of the domestic market. The positioning of each nation can be only approximate, the exact position could be determined just for specific products and the level of technological and managerial resources used to produce them.

One could also postulate that nations move up the bargaining power ladder at different rates. For example, the high speed at which Brazil is acquiring technological and managerial skills, coupled with its educated elite, productive workers and large market, give it a much better bargaining position (and the MNEs much less) than, say, Turkey or Bolivia. Therefore, subsidiaries resident in nations like Brazil or

Figure 8.1: Bargaining Power: National Levels

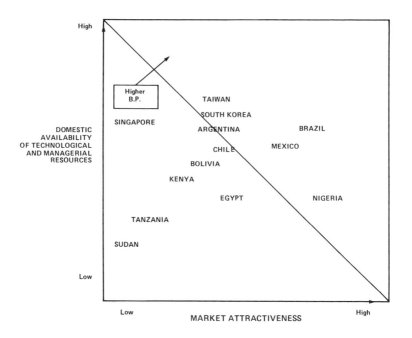

South Korea will have to upgrade their bargaining position frequently. In Brazil, for example, certain segments of the chemical industry have to increase their product selection, level of exports, etc. every three to four years in order to maintain intervention at a low level. Bolivia, on the other hand, does not require anything like that frequency.

Figure 8.2 illustrates the point. The absolute level of bargaining power needed to invest in nations like Bolivia and South Korea is different. The sophistication, complexity and level of technology (all determinants of a firm's bargaining power) necessary for a plant in Bolivia (point A1) can generally be less than that required in a country like South Korea (point A2) to have the same bargaining advantage over domestic interventionists.

The second observation is that because of the higher 'learning' rate in South Korea, its bargaining power rises faster than Bolivia's. This necessitates more frequent bargaining upgrades (point B).

Experience also shows that particular nations not only vary in the

Figure 8.2: Bargaining Power: Rate of Change in Different Nations

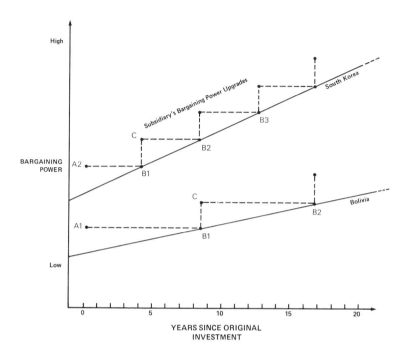

growth of their bargaining power, but perhaps also in the particular *dimension* on which they improve. India, it can be said, has grown quickly in its technological ability but less so in management skills. The opposite may be suggested for a country like the Ivory Coast. Figure 8.3 illustrates this point.

Consequently, MNE subsidiaries find that particular capabilities have a greater effect on intervention in certain nations compared to others. Firms should have products and activities in the Ivory Coast which require a high technological skill level. This would be more effective in reducing intervention than those products which require complex management skills.[2] Similarly, in technologically-able India, less intervention can be expected by firms in which the required management task level is high – and perceived to be high by Indian nationals – or where exports and intra-MNE transfers feature. Examples could include most assembly line operations where poor performance of one task, the

Figure 8.3: Bargaining Power: Nature of Dissipation in Different Nations

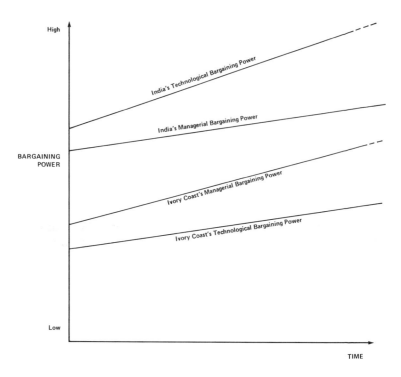

lack of a part, bottlenecks, etc. will stop the entire production. No particular task is complex, but the successful completion of each task in order is.

Variations in Bargaining Behaviour

One other factor that appears to change from nation to nation is the nature of a firm's bargaining *behaviour*. Governments act on their *perception* of the relative bargaining power of state and firm. As mentioned earlier, an important response to intervention is the ability of subsidiary management to communicate the firm's bargaining power and to understand the true intent of domestic interventionist behaviour. The nature of this communication task varies, depending on host country social and political characteristics. For example, competent bargaining activities in the Middle East call for managers with considerable political, rather than engineering or technical, skills.

Other nations call for emphasis on either social, technical or organizational abilities in negotiations.

Neither are host countries always correct in their estimation of their own bargaining power. Countries, like firms, can overestimate their relative bargaining power and strength on a particular dimension (i.e. production technology, market attractiveness, management skill, etc.). It could be suggested that India erred in the late 1970s when it instituted and enforced stringent localization rules against foreign-owned firms. The collective response of the foreign investors in India was to reduce activity, and the inflow of foreign direct investment nearly stopped completely.

Investment Climate

I have spoken little in this book about a nation's investment climate other than in terms of bargaining power and bargaining behaviour. This is partially because I believe much of the information usually involved in descriptions of investment climate have little to do with intervention. In addition to the main determinant of investment, market size (Kobrin, 1976), most of the remaining pertinent host-country information is contained in the data for calculating one's bargaining position. Well-known exceptions would be the nation's trade position, balance of payments and foreign debt position.

In addition to trade and foreign debt data, one unexpected element of the investment climate worth defining is the likely effect of intervention on the activities of other foreign firms. The cost of a single intervention to the host government is compounded when other foreign investors withdraw or delay investment activity because they fear the same experience, or because of concerns over political system instability. The effect is generally greatest in those nations where there is much uncertainty over government policies and political instability. This uncertainty is due mostly to the lack of political track record or political history. Examples would be Papua New Guinea in the early 1970s, post-Manley Jamaica, Singapore in the early 1970s and Turkey of the 1960s.

If you couple this risk of compounding costs of intervention with strong variations in the level of host bargaining power from one industry to the next, the nation's intervention behaviour is not always systematic. Papua New Guinea's bargaining power with respect to foreign mining operations is high, and primarily based on its control over the natural resource after the mine has been established. Its bargaining position in consumer or industrial goods is low, due to a small market and the unavailability of technical and managerial skills. One could argue that Papua New Guinea's hesitancy to exercise the full extent of its power against the mining concerns is due to the damaging effect it could have on subsidiaries in the consumer and industrial goods sectors. Very serious intervention into the mining sector would cause those other subsidiaries to fear greater intervention in their own sector. Because of the high bargaining position of firms in consumer and industrial goods, a perceived threat of greater intervention will result in retaliation or disinvestment by those subsidiaries. In this kind of nation, then, the level of intervention in firms with low bargaining power is often lower than one would expect in other, more typical, countries.

Intervention Management in Different Firms

The feasibility of certain intervention-reducing strategies varies from firm to firm. Wholly foreign-owned subsidiaries of a multi-product MNE have different opportunities to manage intervention than does an MNE involved in a joint venture. Similarly, those MNEs with licensing agreements, management contracts and those which are strategically important have a more limited set of opportunities.

There are several ways one can group or classify firms according to their different approaches to managing intervention. Classifying MNEs according to the extent of product diversification and vertical integration seems to provide a good basis.

The strategies, opportunities, core skills, control system and other characteristics of limited product firms, such as Bata Shoes and Firestone Tire, differ significantly from those of diversified MNEs such as ITT, BAT and Mitsui. Similarly, vertically integrated MNEs such as Alcan, Kimberley-Clark and Goodyear offer opportunities and problems not present in the other kinds of firms.

For each kind of MNE, certain of the strategies for managing intervention introduced in Chapter 6 are more feasible than others. Table 8.1 shows the likely feasibility of the four strategies for each kind of MNE.

It can be seen from Table 8.1 that the limited product MNE has the fewest choices and the most difficult job of reducing intervention. Possibilities of intra-MNE sourcing are low due to the small number of components and the practical requirement that such sourcing be twoway, due to balance-of-payment considerations. Export possibilities vary considerably for this kind of firm.

Some limited product MNEs engage in little international trade

Table 8.1: Feasibility of Intervention Management Strategies

Intervention management strategies	Kind of MNE		
	Limited product MNE	Multi-product MNE	Vertically integrated MNE
New processes	High	Moderate	Moderate
New products	Low	High	Low-Moderate
Exports	Low-High	Low-Moderate	Low-Moderate
Intra-MNE sourcing	Low	Moderate	High

operating instead behind tariff walls, establishing miniature replicas of the parent in each nation. Many limited product MNEs, however, are world traders supplying their many markets from central production points. These MNEs have the requisite amount of resources and skills to build world-scale competitive plants anywhere in the world where input costs permit.

Multi-product MNEs have a slight advantage over others because of the greater choice of opportunities available to improve their bargaining position. While their main advantage derives from their ability to introduce new products this advantage is more vulnerable over time than is the key to the success of the vertically integrated MNEs: intra-MNE sourcing. No single corporate activity deters intervention more than intra-MNE sourcing, be it dry-cell batteries from a Japanese subsidiary in Tanzania or components from the Ford plant in Brazil.

The utility of this sourcing strategy across the three different kinds of MNEs will increase if the trend towards global products continues. Global products such as automobiles, cameras, VCRs, stereos and some packaged food products, open up new possibilities for intra-MNE sourcing. Components as well as end products become almost identical thereby increasing the likelihood that the production of products and components can take place in two or three places in the world. Instead of unique products being produced in each major market, a single product with superior generic quality and low price takes their place. Exploiting the economies of scale in production, and perhaps R & D and product management, subsidiaries will now be able to specialize in one or two products for a wide geographic area, importing the remainder of its product line needs from an associated subsidiary. (For details on global products and global firms see Levitt, 1983.)

While strictly not a type of MNE, joint ventures are a frequent, if not always desirable, form of international investment. The term joint venture has been used rather loosely, however, to describe quite different kinds of activities. Some joint ventures have a 'silent' partner with no involvement in operations other than receipt of a dividend cheque. Other joint ventures have the partners operating different functions of the firm, interacting daily in the pursuit of shared and individual goals. Here I am referring to the true joint venture, where two or more partners – domestic and foreign – share in the operation of the joint enterprise.

In terms of managing intervention, joint ventures are a special case due to the presence of domestic shareholders or independent managers within the operation of the firm. Either or both of these domestic groups could find intervention worth promoting or supporting. This occurs primarily because most joint ventures provide an ideal opportunity for MNE-based managerial and technological skills to be transferred to the domestic partner or to the joint venture management. New production processes are understood more quickly by domestic managers on the scene, and management skills are obtained either through on-the-job training or formal courses offered by the foreign partner.

The likelihood of intervention in joint ventures is a function of the speed of technology transfer, and the foreign control over the joint venture management. Because of its complexity or speed of change, some skills and technologies are slow to transfer, even in joint ventures. The main point is that, ceteris paribis, the joint venture form of investment reduces more rapidly the MNE's bargaining power. The argument that the joint venture satiates the host partner's – or his government's – interventionist desires has no precedent in corporate or political behaviour.

The issue of who controls those joint venture managers and technicians who learn or absorb the MNE-supplied technology also determines the amount of intervention. In cases where the large majority of such people are supplied by, or under the control of, the MNE there is reduced risk of the joint venture management colluding with the domestic partner to increase their share of the venture's profits. When management is controlled by the domestic partner or is neutral, the risks are of course higher.

As a consequence, joint ventures provide more limited opportunities for the management of intervention. Intervention management policies calling for new processes or products are much less effective unless they are coupled with control over senior joint venture managers and technicians. Using the control mechanism as a means of maintaining bargaining power has its own costs, however. Work on a joint venture performance by Killing (1982, 1983), Schaan (1983) and Beamish (1984) has shown how MNE insistence on controlling joint venture management may cause poor performance when joint ventures are in the newly-industrialized countries such as Mexico and Brazil, and an even greater probability of poor performance in the lesser-developed countries. Generally, the amount of control each partner exerts and the activities controlled should reflect the skills and resources each party brings to the joint venture. In Brazil, for example, no single party can usually control the venture overall due to the need for technical input (MNE) and Brazilian marketing and political input. In most LDCs, especially where competition is slight, operating control by the domestic partner or a host-nation executive often provides the appropriate mix of core skills in the venture.

The only strategies readily available to joint venture MNEs wishing to manage intervention without rapid and costly changes in process and products are the latter two mentioned in Table 8.1: increasing exports to unrelated firms, and increasing intra-MNE sourcing. The power and efficacy of exporting and, in particular, sourcing, are generally not reduced by the joint venture form of investment. The power of the exporting strategy may be diluted when export success is not determined by MNE-based market information, marketing and sales assistance, but by skills resident in joint venture management. Intra-firm sourcing by its very nature is controlled by the MNE, and hence forms the fundamental strategy for managing intervention.

For firms involved in the licensing of technology or management contracting, intervention exists in the form of premature contract cancellation or non-payment. To reduce the likelihood or severity of such intervention, such international firms have little option other than the rather obvious control over the supply of needed technology and managerial skills, the significance of which is determined by its proprietory nature. Tactics such as purposefully slowing down or retarding the transfer of such skills to local staff, or artificially increasing the firm's significance, appear to be effective only in the short term and can quickly become known to potential customers in other countries.

Strategically Important MNEs

Finally, how do intervention-prone, strategically important firms manage intervention? Firms with a high political and strategic profile in mining, farming, public utilities, very large firms, etc. experience high intervention with only little regard to their bargaining strength as we have defined it. The political and sometimes economic consequences are so large that the incentive to intervene often takes precedent over the economic costs of such intervention. As a consequence, the four strategies for increasing bargaining power discussed in the previous sections are not as productive or effective in the case of strategic industries.

Instead, such firms have attempted to manage intervention in two related ways: by reducing the assets at stake or the extent of their risks, and by increasing the costs of intervention through the broad involvement of investing firms and nations.

Both these approaches are incorporated in the structure of many strategic investments and can be illustrated by examining the nature of a recent mining investment. The objective of the major investor – a mining firm – was to utilize both of the above approaches by involving as many investors from as many nations as possible. The mine operator was a Belgian firm; the supplier of capital for the infrastructure was a multilateral agency. West German and Swiss machinery was purchased, financed by those countries' respective export finance organizations; and, finally, the main customer was Japanese who also financially supported the operation.

Because of this strategy, the financial risks were spread among five groups and any serious intervention was at the cost of annoying four strong nations plus a multilateral agency. That is not to say that intervention would not occur. It could, especially if the host government was confident it would not be so severe as to warrant government-to-government disagreement. But with this organizational structure, severe intervention would attract equally widespread and possibly severe retribution. The fact that the shareholding is so widespread also deters the intervening nation from switching its allegiance from one home country to another in order to find a new patron.

Project finance syndicated among several agencies and nationals also creates a similar transnational web to raise the costs of intervention. While this type of deterrent is subject to much criticism from the host governments, its use is reportedly growing in frequency (see Moran, 1981, 1983). The only alternative for many MNEs is not to invest at all because their operations have such a high political profile that no other defence has any material effect.

Summary and Conclusion

Previous chapters have shown how each MNE's preferred strategy of intervention management is a function of specific company and host-nation factors. One can carefully limit the feasible set of strategies, however, by considering particular kinds of host countries and MNEs.

Host nations vary significantly on three dimensions of interest to the intervention manager: the absolute national level of bargaining power; the speed of increase; and the speed of bargaining power improvement on various dimensions, i.e. technology or management skills. To the MNE, these national differences result in radically different approaches to intervention management. Some subsidiaries will require state-of-the-art technologies with frequent upgrades, involving technical or managerial complexity. Other subsidiaries of the same MNE can utilize less complex operations and products and require only infrequent modifications to the original investment.

The smooth upward progression of host-nation technological and managerial learning curves can not always be relied upon, however. Brazil does not progress from manufacturing wrenches and light switches to aircraft and digital chips over a ten-year period without significant external help. The growth of international consultants, and of firms willing to license the latest technology and then train host companies to manage it successfully is beginning to play a significant role in several nations. Their activities are felt by MNEs who experience increased intervention because of the dramatic jump in host-nation 'capabilities' they create.

The firm's preferred strategy for reducing intervention is influenced by company and industry factors. Limited product, multi-product and vertically-integrated MNEs differ on several dimensions of interest to the intervention manager: opportunities for implementing the four main intervention-reducing strategies, corporate skills and weaknesses and the competitive environment. A consideration of those dimensions shows that limited product MNEs are highly dependent on new processes and export strategies, multi-product MNEs have a greater choice of strategies highlighted by new product opportunities, while vertically-integrated MNEs can rely on intra-MNE sourcing and new process innovations. The growth of global products will provide ever greater opportunities for the strongest deterrent to intervention, intra-MNE sourcing.

Two other kinds of multinationals are those involved in joint ventures and in strategically important industries. Joint ventures are characterized by the high degree of skill and technology transfer that takes place between MNE and the joint venture partner and/or venture management. Consequently, intervention strategies of new processes and products have less utility due to the higher speed at which the MNE's 'advantage' is dissipated. For most joint ventures, then, the most effective intervention strategies are exporting and intra-MNE sourcing. Unambiguous MNE dominance over joint venture management increases the feasibility of using the other defensive strategies.

Involvement in strategically important industries severely limits the use of the main intervention-reducing strategies introduced here. Experience shows that the only strategy requires structuring the ownership, financing and marketing of the venture so that several national interests are involved. Under most conditions, this will increase the cost of intervention to the host nation and, at worst, provide the MNE with some reduction of its asset exposure.

Notes

1. For a description of the determinants of market attractiveness see *Business International*, 6 January 1984, p. 8.

2. Complexity of management skills can be described by the number, difficulty and interrelationship of management decisions required to produce a product.

9 MANAGING INTERVENTION: THE MNE PARENT ORGANIZATION

If the management of intervention at the level of the subsidiary is some-what straightforward, the collective response of the multinational enterprise is not. In order to be effective, the management of intervention must be an integrated part of the normal decision-making of the MNE. Successful worldwide management of intervention also requires particular management skills. And finally, the most difficult aspect of intervention management must be overcome by MNE management: intervention management requires behaviour almost completely opposite to tradition. Instead of reducing the assets and resources exposed to likely intervention, successful management now necessitates policies which often increase asset exposure.

In this chapter, we shall examine these intervention management issues from the perspective of the MNE parent attempting to implement a worldwide system of intervention management. Realistically, MNEs will not change dramatically their existing processes and organization to accommodate a new activity (Galbraith and Nathanson, 1978; March and Simon, 1958). Therefore, successful implementation will involve integrating intervention management into the existing operational decision-making and planning processes.

Initially, this chapter will review some of the more general issues of worldwide implementation and integration. Next, the specific managerial issues associated with the four strategies for increasing bargaining power will be discussed. Finally, we shall review the implications these activities have for other MNE policies and strategies.

Strategic Implementation and Integration: Some General Issues

Successful management of intervention throughout a multinational's worldwide organization requires that a number of significant decisions be made. Products get assigned, export markets are allocated and capital projects are approved. All of these are decisions which generally have some impact on all the MNEs' subsidiaries. In addition, the allocation of resources to reduce intervention is determined on the basis of relative need: the need for one subsidiary's bargaining power upgrade as compared to all other subsidiaries in the MNE.

The reason why successful implementation of an intervention management strategy requires integration into the normal decision-making and planning activities of the MNE lies in the number and complexity of intervention decisions. Through integration, intervention management would form part of the normal capital allocation, personnel planning and strategic planning processes, and would not be an activity performed by individuals in staff positions isolated from operational decision-making.

The tendency for new criteria or perspective to be isolated from normal decision-making is not unusual. Attempts by MNEs and domestic firms to integrate ethical standards and evaluation techniques into corporate decision-making has generally met with little success. Kobrin (1982) reports a similar fate with the use of risk (political instability) analysis and data. These activities often get assigned to departments or individuals who are members of corporate staff and not line management. These individuals tend to generate copious amounts of data and scenarios, which may be accurate, but nevertheless are seldom integrated into the corporate planning process.

The reason for the lack of successful integration is that line managers and decision-makers are uncertain how to use the information provided. This situation is often due to the form of the data. Managers can understand, for example, that there may be questions raised on the moral and ethical standards involved in operations in a particular host nation. They also realize that the same ethical standard is often the norm in this particular country, and that it is impossible to do business there and avoid it. Given this kind of data, then, the decision-maker finds considerable difficulty in utilizing the information in his decision to invest.

Similar integration problems occur when raw environmental data such as balance of payments figures, trade union activity, the influence of various political ideologies and the like are presented to MNE managers. When the investment decision must be made and — as is usually the case — alternative locations are found to have political environment and market desirability data which make them roughly comparable sites, the decision-maker does not know what to do further with such data to help him make better decisions.

It appears that successful integration of information into the normal decision-making process of the MNE requires that the data be presented in a form which readily indicates preferred policy alternatives or new courses of action. This outcome is achieved through either early incorporation of the data by the decision-makers into their policy alternatives, or, by having the data presented by staff specialists so that specific actions are clear to managers. There are trade-offs. For the line decision-makers to incorporate such data successfully, a strong familiarity with the information, its source, implications and weaknesses is required. Staff specialists, while they have a better knowledge of the subject matter, find it difficult to see what the effect will be on corporate practices of which they understand relatively little.

While it is nor clear whether the staff or line approach is the best for all circumstances, it seems fairly obvious that the more complex the external data, the more appropriate staff specialists would be. A second factor especially relevant in the case of intervention management has to do with the source of such external data. Intervention data are not universally available, unlike trade balances and country indebtness. Instead, they are country- and firm-specific, with the subsidiary's management best able to provide and evaluate such data.[1] The trade-offs then are not simple, and are dealt with below.

In addition to defining the location of the intervention management function, successful integration is also influenced by the process of information collection. The nature of this communication process is very much a function of the MNE's organizational structure. Geographic area structures provide different avenues of communications than product line organizations. Consequently, this chapter will also discuss the appropriateness of various organizational structures to the management of intervention.

Intervention Management: the Management Process

Managing intervention successfully within the MNE involves a process that can be divided into four activities. Each activity is distinct and requires different sets of skills and capabilities. The four activities are as follows:

1. *Data Collection*
   * need and timing of each subsidiary's bargaining power upgrade,
   * feasible set of intervention management strategies for each subsidiary,
   * a cost-benefit analysis of each strategy;

2. *Analysis and Decision*

* construction of a hierarchy of subsidiaries needing bargaining up-grades,
* availability of MNE capital resources compared to subsidiary needs,
* availability of new technology and products for overseas production,
* decisions on specific activities for each subsidiary with an implementation timetable;

3. *Implementation*

* transfer and utilization of new activities to each subsidiary,
* changes in levels of training, competence, staffing and tenure of appointment to implement the new strategy,
* new roles for home and area offices in transferring technology and management skill at the higher rate;

4. *Integration*

* co-ordinating intra-MNE sourcing and export flows,
* re-establishing new levels of integration and differentiation between parent MNE and subsidiary.

In the following sections each activity will be described.

1. *Data Collection*

Two main activities describe this aspect of the intervention management process: the specification of the subsidiary's need for a bargaining power upgrade, and determining the appropriateness and desirability of each of the four strategies for increasing bargaining power.

The first activity has been described in detail in Chapters 7 and 8. Data on each subsidiary's bargaining power compared to that of its host nation and possible competitors are obtained by each subsidiary in the manner outlined earlier.

For the MNE interested in obtaining such information from all its subsidiaries it is important that the data are comparable, and that common terms and measurements are used by all subsidiaries. Without this requirement, the job of allocating resources among the subsidiaries becomes impossible.

This is where the staff specialist can play a major role: through training and the establishment of appropriate processes and systems common to all subsidiaries. The subsidiary manager responsible for such data collection can be trained in the necessary evaluation techniques, and reporting forms can be devised which will allow comparability of data, some rigidity of terminology and ensure that all the data needed are collected, along with the usual quality checks.

This process and the role of the staff specialist find an analogy in the capital budgeting process of most firms. Training sessions are held frequently and reporting forms are prescribed along with reporting frequencies. The staff specialist defines the reporting activities of the line personnel, but does not provide input *nor* does he establish a hierarchical relationship with the subsidiary manager. Any reports that do find their way to the specialist are not used to make decisions on the capital request per se, but to monitor the accuracy of reporting procedure.

While the above data can come directly from the subsidiary's executive group, the relative appropriateness of each of the four intervention-reducing strategies for a particular subsidiary poses a more difficult problem. Each of the intervention-reducing strategies introduced in this book requires somewhat different sets of technical and managerial skills to be implemented successfully. Therefore, the MNE parent needs to know – objectively – about the relative strengths and weaknesses of each subsidiary in order to evaluate the likelihood of successful implementation by the subsidiary.

While the specific nature of the skills required by each strategy varies from company to company, some generalizations can still be made. New manufacturing processes (but keeping the same product(s)) usually emphasize production skills, maintenance skills and the availability of foreign exchange for the new machinery. The successful introduction of new products requires general management and marketing skills, some technical skill and extra capacity. Exports require world-scale cost structures, cheap access to international transportation, access to international marketing expertise and, in general, an efficient organization of the type not normally found in subsidiaries operating in protected economies. Finally, intra-MNE sourcing requires logistics controls, the ability to implement company-wide technical standards and product specifications, and production cost control.

The data needed to select the strategy appropriate to the subsidiary are, then, the relative technical and managerial strengths of the subsidiary, its cost structure – partially determined by its environment – and the likelihood of change in all of these characteristics. Obtaining impartial estimates of these data from the subsidiary is rather difficult: underestimating areas of weakness and overestimating one's abilities to learn new skills is endemic to most executives.

Here, one has to rely on either corporate staff or other line managers to provide input, in addition to subsidiary management. As we will see later on in this section, the geographic area office or the product-line group responsible for the subsidiary are ideal sources for this data.

Operationally, the output of this activity will be an evaluation of each of the four strategies for each subsidiary. For example, a subsidiary operating in a highly protected, high-cost nation would tend to evaluate more highly the new processes and new product alternatives rather than the exporting and sourcing options. Under each strategy, one could conduct a feasibility study outlining the subsidiary's expected profit and the commensurate risk attached.

2. Analysis and Decision

The next stage in the intervention management process is aggregating the data mentioned above, collecting additional data, analyzing them and finally deciding on the intervention management strategies to be followed by each subsidiary. First, however, comes the question of locating this function. Who should perform this analysis and who should recommend or make the final decision on each subsidiary's intervention strategy?

Some assistance in answering this question can be had by examining what we know about the organizational structures of international and domestic firms and the determinants of these structures. From the work of Stopford and Wells (1972), Davis (1975, 1976), and others, we know that firms change their organizational structures in response to certain factors in order to obtain better decision-making and control by senior line and staff managers. One factor determining the appropriate structure is the level of decision-making complexity facing senior managers. Simply put, high levels of complexity result in organizational change which either reduces the scope of the job or, alternatively, moves the decision point closer to the source of the complexity or uncertainty – usually the market place. Here, the level of decision-making is determined by three things:

1. the experience of the firm with similar business problems;
2. the speed of change in the corporate (internal) and external environments;
3. the number of different circumstances (the span of control) the executive must address, for example, number of products, countries, etc.

The other factor one addresses when considering organizational structure is the decision-maker's access to and control over the business' key success factors. For example, if a critical factor is a quick transfer of standard product, technical and marketing information to all subsidiaries with little modifications to the local market, then most decision-making power will be centralized at the parent firm with direct subsidiary-parent reporting procedures. If, on the other hand, products must be significantly adapted to local markets, more decision-making power will be decentralized and given to subsidiary managers. If there are economies to be made by co-ordinating production, transport, and sales by region, then power will be given to an area office to carry out this function.

Applying these two factors to the case of managing intervention, we find that centralizing intervention analysis and decision-making at the MNE parent would not likely be appropriate. Instead, decentralizing such decisions appears to be suggested by the nature of the intervention problems. First, the analysis of intervention data is very complex: the data are subsidiary and host nation-specific, so the number of situations is large; much of the data is subjectively derived and hence more complex; and many executives have little experience in this matter. These facts suggest that the locus of the analyst and the decision-maker be 'lower' down the organization, so as to permit a more narrow span of control (i.e. a manageable set of nations and subsidiaries), and to reduce the number of levels between the analyst decision-maker and the subsidiary.

The second element influencing the organizational structure does not provide such a clear signal. While the need to accurately monitor each subsidiary's bargaining position and that of his host nation suggests decentralized decision-making, the selection of a specific strategy for increasing bargaining power favours centralization. Both the new product and process strategies suggest a decision-maker who is aware of all MNE products, and new processes: the MNE parent. Furthermore, exporting and especially intra-MNE sourcing require co-ordination which is much better done at the parent rather than in a decentralized office.

For certain kinds of MNEs, the solution does not require too much compromise between the above two considerations. Those MNEs with many subsidiaries in a given geographical area — say a firm with 20 subsidiaries in the Indian Ocean and South East Asia region — will find that the co-ordination function is far better done at the regional level rather than at the parent. The size and large number of subsidiaries in such an area permit an area office of significant size and skill to manage the necessary co-ordination and analytical functions, and at the same time to acquire information on available MNE technology and products. Hence, for this kind of MNE the intervention analysis and decision-making function is best located at the area office.

Those firms with relatively few subsidiaries are generally organized with an international division separate from the dominant domestic operations of the firm.[2] This kind of MNE seldom has an area office of much significance and authority and, therefore, almost by default the intervention management function falls to the international division headquarters staff.

The other extreme is occupied by the MNE with a worldwide product-line organization that does not discriminate organizationally between home and overseas markets. For these MNEs without any geographic area organization whatsoever, the management of intervention can be perhaps most difficult. As long as new product upgrades and intra-MNE sourcing is possible within the same division the problem is easily handled. It is when products from other divisions are involved that communications from subsidiary 'A' to division 'A' to division 'B' to subsidiary 'B' become, not surprisingly, very cumbersome.

Many such world-product division MNEs have found it useful to have some sort of area co-ordination function. This resultant organization structure approaches a matrix format.[3] (European MNEs and most service and financial MNEs are frequent users of this structure, but US manufacturing MNEs such as ITT and others also utilize it.) In these cases the analytical, decision-making and, as we will see later in this chapter, the co-ordination functions are best performed at the area co-ordinating office rather than at the parent or by the product-line organization.

Having discussed the locus of the intervention analysis and decision-making function, we can now turn to specifying the management activities involved. The first step calls for the construction of a hierarchy of subsidiaries with reference to their need for bargaining power upgrades. For each subsidiary on the list, three items of data will be needed:

* the amount of upgrade (major, moderate, minor) necessary;
* the kind of upgrade preferred (sourcing, new products, etc.) and,
* the time at which the upgrade is needed.

Having established the 'demand' side of the upgrades necessary, the intervention manager will then create a summary of the 'supply' of intervention-reducing strategies within the MNE. As established earlier in this book, intervention-reducing strategies require four types of resources; capital, product and process technology, export markets and management skill. In the majority of MNEs, these resources are in limited supply and, during certain periods, particular resources may be completely unavailable. Before there can be a matching of supply and demand, the intervention manager has to construct a list of as many resources as he can obtain from his division, the parent, or from external sources.

For certain kinds of resources drafting such a list poses few problems. Procedures are well established within MNEs to establish the availability of capital for such intervention-reducing activities as product addition utilizing the existing portfolio of MNE products. While not as well established, procedures also exist outlining the availability of *new* products and processes from the same division. Interesting products and processes from other divisions, or all products and processes in the case of geographic area organizations, are not readily made available to those who have to manage intervention.

As a result, the intervention manager must create new procedures within the MNE to keep him aware of the MNE's supply of opportunities for satisfying its subsidiaries' intervention management needs. Strict lines of divisional control over products and markets may have to be relaxed in order to supply a subsidiary in division A, for example, with compatible products from division B.

The most difficult set of opportunities for the intervention manager to supply is the feasible set of export markets for particular products. In this context, such markets would be ones not already served by the subsidiary; but there may be a sister subsidiary operating there selling other products. Using these contacts to identify export market opportunities for another subsidiary has had some small success in certain MNEs. Generally, it is up to the exporting subsidiary or specialist staff group to find such opportunities rather than to rely on them being reported by other parts of the MNE.

Similar sets of problems exist in locating opportunities for intra-MNE sourcing of components, raw materials and finished products. If this matching process of finding sourcing suppliers and receivers takes place outside MNE strategic planning and the capital budgeting process, the possibilities of success are somewhat remote. Questions over sourcing are long-term ones which are taken into account early in the planning process. Consequently, when the intervention-reducing benefits of such sourcing become part of the formulation activities of an international production strategy, the integration problem is reduced. Certain subsidiaries are given the mandate for producing standard components for all subsidiaries in that region, or even worldwide if transportation economies allow. Firms such as Black & Decker and IBM are both good examples of this approach.

The process of identifying new product processes, export markets and especially sourcing opportunities underlines the importance of the intervention management function being integrated into line strategic planning and the capital allocation procedures. Because strategy setting and capital control are indivisible in most firms, this is the same process with a single executive responsible for both activities.

Returning to the managerial activities required at this stage, now that the executive has listings of both subsidiary needs for bargaining upgrades and the availability of these upgrades within the MNE system, a matching process occurs. The result would be a statement of planned intervention management activities for all the subsidiaries involved over the firm's planning period. All subsidiaries and not just those requesting upgrades must be involved, because solutions such as sourcing, etc. generally affect more than one subsidiary. A component sourced from one subsidiary to increase its bargaining power also provides some protection to the receiving subsidiary.

The planning horizon used by several MNEs is sometimes quite long, say, ten to fifteen years. One of the reasons for this is the sometimes long duration of bargaining upgrades in certain nations with little bargaining power. Another reason is the long-term effect of certain strategies. A decision to push exports as a basic strategy for minimizing intervention in subsidiary A for several planning periods has a finite life. Eventually, that subsidiary will have to start sourcing or producing new products, etc. The long-term planning process should provide for products and sourcing opportunities to be made available at that future date by co-ordinating planning.

Table 9.1 illustrates a ten-year intervention management plan for a US-based MNE in the consumer goods business. The coverage is for the Indian Ocean planning sector. A point to note is that the plan attempts to avoid introductions of new products or processes in more than one subsidiary per year because of the pressure this would place on parent company management. Similarly, new sourcing activities — all twoway in this case, due to endemic foreign exchange problems — are well spaced out where possible, for similar reasons.

Table 9.1: Intervention Management Plan for Indian Ocean Group

Subsidiary	1983	1984	1985	1986	TEN-YEAR PLAN 1987	1988	1989	1990	1991	1992
A India[b]	5[a]	5	4	3 sourcing with F	6	6	5	4	3 new processes	5
B Singapore	5	4	4	3 new process	5	4	4	3 sourcing H and I	6	5
C Thailand	4	4	3 export to USA, Oceana	6	5	5	4	4	3 sourcing E now F 1992	6
D Indonesia	3 export to C and F	5	4	4	3 new process	5	4	4	3 new product	4
E Philippines	6	5	5	5	4	4	4	3	3 sourcing with C now and F 1993	6
F Australia	5	4	4	3 sourcing with A	6	5	5	4	3	5 sourcing with C
G Egypt	6	6	5	5	4	4 export Middle East and Mediterranean	6	5	5	5
H Kenya	4	4	3 new products	5	5	5	4	3 sourcing B	6	5
I South Africa	3 new product and processes	5	5	5	4	4	3	3 sourcing B	6	6

Notes: a. Numbers represent the relative bargaining power of each subsidiary in each country, each year. A source of 3 means the firm has the same bargaining power as the host nation; 4 slightly more; 5 much more; and 6 complete. See Chapter 7 for details.
b. Bargaining power dissipates in certain nations faster than others due to country's learning rate and bargaining power changes. For this area, those nations which caused the firm's bargaining power to dissipate faster were India and Indonesia. Moderate dissipators were Thailand, Singapore, Australia and Kenya. Nations where the firm's bargaining power has reduced slowly were the Philippines, Egypt and South Africa.

The bargaining power figures used in the exhibit are derived in a fashion similar to those introduced in Chapter 7, rounded to the lowest whole number. When the rating for each subsidiary is forecast to be a 3 (actually anywhere between 3.0 and 3.9), which represents a level of bargaining power equal to the host nation's, the MNE plans an upgrade of some sort. This particular firm expects a larger proportion of its products to be global by the early 1990s. As a result it is planning to centrally manufacture products for several nations by that time. This will permit significant amounts of intra-firm sourcing during that period. Should the global product forecast not come true, the firm has plans for investment computer-aided design and manufacturing (CAD/CAM) which will it is hoped allow the efficient manufacture of several different products, i.e. short runs as compared to manufacturing global products. The strong interest of this MNE in ensuring that sourcing will exist is because of their view that such strong deterrents against intervention will be necessary in *their* subsidiaries after 1990. This is due to their forecast of increasing host-nation capabilities and the popularity of licensing by North American, European and Japanese firms who specialize in licensing and not foreign direct investment.

3. Implementation

Implementing the strategy is essentially a problem of transferring the new technology or skills required to the subsidiary. This problem can be further divided into two components: the actual transfer from parent MNE to the subsidiary, and the preparation of subsidiary management to utilize effectively the new technology.

The actual transfer of these widely defined capabilities is a step in the intervention management programme which MNEs have few difficulties. The primary national for the multinational enterprise is its efficient development and exchange of capabilities (material, financial, strategic, technical and human) between the parent and the subsidiaries. Many capabilities are more difficult to transfer than others, however. These tend to be competences or skills unique to individuals or groups. The blueprints and dies needed to produce a type of product can be relatively easily transferred. On the other hand, MNEs find that transferring the competence to solve complex local marketing problems or to develop another product requires different and complex organizational mechanisms.

Capabilities reside within a particular unit or group of people. For example, all the information (technical, production, marketing, sales, etc.) on a new product usually resides in the product group where it originated — frequently in the home nation. Transferring this knowledge to another group is costly to the originating group: time and effort must be spent formulating the information in such a way that it can be easily communicated to outsiders; the outsiders must be informed, trained and helped; problems the recipients encounter in implementation have to be discussed and resolved.

To offset these transfer costs to the holders of the capability, MNEs provide incentives which reduce the cost. Poynter and White (1984) noted that, for example, some MNEs reward the part of the firm owning technology on the basis of worldwide profits from their technology; other MNEs establish a strictly enforced system of technology reciprocity. Others force the transfer through stimulation of senior managers coupled with corporate philosophies which instigate and reward such sharing behaviour.

In the case of transferring new product or process technology to overseas subsidiaries, one of these incentive mechanisms has to be in place. This is especially so in the case of small and distant subsidiaries where the managers are often from a different culture than the home nation's. Here the costs of transferring technology are even higher.

While MNEs have considerable experience in transferring capabilities, the preparation of the recipient subsidiary to acquire and successfully implement the new technology poses a greater challenge. Intervention management results in more complex capabilities being transferred with an equal need for more competent subsidiary executives. The transfer for the latest manufacturing process and a state of-the-art product, and the requirement to manufacture, finish and ship a component to exact specifications and to a rigid timetable is quite a shock to a subsidiary used to manufacturing in a protected domestic market a mature product using de-bugged machinery employed by the parent for many years.

Not only does the subsidiary's level of technical, production and marketing expertise need to rise but their problem-solving skill too. New products and processes come from the parent with many questions on reliability, product-market positioning, etc. still unanswered. In general, success can be achieved by more training, better personnel and greater regard for competent overseas personnel. The last comment is especially pertinent for US MNEs who, like a few others, do not place great emphasis on the management quality in their subsidiaries. For many firms, subsidiaries are often used as training grounds for home-nation executives. Whether this may or may not be appropriate to existing circumstances is difficult to judge. However, with the higher rate of technology transfers that comes with the management of intervention, greater emphasis will be placed on managerial competence. That fact, coupled with the demands for efficient production required for exporting and sourcing, may suggest some changes in MNE personnel policies.

4. Integration

The final managerial action required to successfully manage intervention is the integration of all the subsidiary-based intervention strategies and the management of any side effects this increased inter-dependence may produce. As mentioned earlier, the main strategies requiring integration and co-ordination are sourcing and exports. Sourcing activities usually cannot be easily co-ordinated by the subsidiaries involved, especially when disputes over pricing and supply arise. Exports, marketing and sales, too, are often beyond the normal capabilities of subsidiaries which are used to operating in one country.

The solutions adopted by MNEs again vary in line with their organizational structure. Large, multi-product MNEs have established coordinating bodies and in-house trading groups to handle export sales. Others find these roles taken over by the geographic area office or, for those with worldwide product division structures, by a specialist staff group.

A more difficult problem arises as a result of this greater integration and the resultant reduction of subsidiary autonomy. This usually has two costs: it often makes it more difficult for the subsidiary to react to local environmental stimuli; and the reduction of autonomy, if not offset with greater managerial challenges or rewards elsewhere, can have a negative effect on executive morale and productivity. (For further discussions on strategies for subsidiaries see Prahalad and Doz, 1981, and Poynter and White, 1984.)

This problem of trading-off the benefits to be had from integration in an increasingly competitive and world-scale oriented market, with the costs from being unable to easily respond to the domestic environment in a world characterized with increasing host-government intervention, is complex and not easily solved. Mutually obtaining both an integrated and differentiated strategy appropriate to one's particular host country often proves to be organizationally weak. Matrix-type organizations provide some success, but only a minority of MNEs have been able to implement this organizational form successfully.

Managing Intervention: Operational Progress

Putting this strategy for managing intervention into operation has been a slow process with some unexpected problems and benefits. A few MNEs have adopted the approach worldwide, others are testing it in particular geographic areas. Many firms implicitly adopt parts of the strategy as they struggle to maintain their level of profits and risk in subsidiary operations. By monitoring the successes and failures of firms it appears that the main difficulties are of two kinds: first, complications arise from the fact that actions which follow from this strategy run completely counter to the MNE's traditional response to intervention; and, second, the scarcity of personnel appropriate to the new strategy.

The intervention strategies call for more managerial and technical capabilities to be located in subsidiaries. Not only do export strategies, technology upgrades and intra-MNE sourcing call for more technical skills, but — as all observers of the international scene suggest — increased numbers of politically-attuned executives can be profitably used in subsidiaries, too. The high cost of the former, and the scarcity of the latter, deter some MNEs.

This disadvantage is not equal in all MNEs, however. Some MNEs appear to have far fewer problems in obtaining executives willing to spend most of their careers in subsidiaries. While the source of the inequality is not yet clear, differences in control systems, executive recruitment policies, promotion patterns and perceived subsidiary autonomy are often mentioned.

The apparent difficulties of acquiring and keeping politically-attuned executives also appear to be unequally spread among MNEs. More accurately, there is a strong suggestion that most MNEs have great difficulties managing technologically-adept executives along with politically-adept ones in the same organization. It appears that organizational structures, promotion and reporting relationships and the dictates of corporate strategy cannot easily adjust to having such diametrically-opposed executives. In a technology-driven MNE, executives with considerable political or country-based skills inevitably find themselves in ineffective staff positions. Such executives seem to be more active, and hold line positions, in MNEs where knowledge of domestic markets, distribution channels, etc. is the driving force behind the company — as in the consumer packaged foods industry, for example.

While the market-driven firms seem to be the main benefactors of the politically-adept executives, the technology-driven MNEs do not necessarily seem to suffer from increased intervention. The answer of course lies in the latter's use of changing technology as a source of bargaining power, a defence infrequently used by market-driven firms. Many traditional US (technology-driven) and UK (market-driven) MNEs illustrate the differences between the two types of MNEs.

The second factor which complicates MNE attempts to implement the intervention strategy is the complete reversal it represents from the traditional MNE response to intervention. For much of their history, when threatened, most MNEs responded by *reducing* their asset exposure, speeding up profit repatriation and taking out 'unnecessary' executives. This response was justified in light of the highly unpredictable nature of government intervention, and because it also paralleled the behaviour – and won the approval – of international bankers.

While this strategy may conceivably still apply to banks with international exposures, it no longer does for MNEs. Instead, subsidiary defence strategies call for *increased* investment when intervention threatens. Multinationals wishing to avoid costly intervention do so by staying ahead of the capabilities of domestic interventionists, and not by competing head on or by running away.

The strategic shift required by the new intervention strategy brings with it the usual executive behaviour which accompanies change. Executives tend to concentrate on the negative aspects associated with the shift: the decreased profit margins from the export compared to domestic market; the high capital requirements of new products and processes; the personnel problem associated with longer overseas postings; and the like.

The costs of the intervention management strategy are more easily identified and quantified than are the benefits. The costs are the result of management actions, around which there is little uncertainty – for MNE executives. The benefits to be derived from these investments are external to the firm and far more uncertain, determined by the modified behaviour of host-nation groups. When costs are perceived to be certain and benefits uncertain – although undeniably high – the organization has a built-in hesitancy to change. While this reaction is a healthy one, it slows down the implementation of strategies such as this.

Summary and Conclusion

This chapter is concerned with the management issues that arise in the MNE parent as they attempt to formulate and implement a worldwide system of intervention management. Overriding these recommendations is the fact that experience shows that new activities such as intervention management have to fit into existing organizational and decision-making arrangements of the MNE in order to be effective. While the existing organizational structure may not be optimal, organizations do not easily change structures to accommodate new activities. Consequently, the recommendations concentrate on integrating intervention management into existing capital budgeting and strategy-making processes.

The successful management of intervention involves four successive activities: data collection, analysis and decision-making, implementation, and integration. The *data collection* phase produces the needs and timing for each subsidiary, the feasible set of strategies and their cost and benefit. This activity is best performed by subsidiary personnel with training support by staff specialists.

The second activity of *analysis and decision-making* produces a matching of subsidiary needs or resources with the availability of these resources (e.g. new products, export markets, etc.) within the MNE — unusually difficult in worldwide product division MNEs — and, finally, a timetable of intervention — reducing strategies for all subsidiaries. Table 9.1 provided an example of such a timetable. The preferred location of this activity is fairly low in the organization.

The *implementation* phase covers the successful transfer of the new strategy to the subsidiary. This involves not only the preparation of subsidiary personnel for successful implementation, which requires training, a longer term overseas, etc., but also an organizational structure which facilitates the rapid and successful transfer of technology or managerial skill from subsidiary to subsidiary, and from division to division. This activity suggests new roles for home and area offices.

The *integration* phase represents the co-ordination activities for sourcing and exports, and includes management problems that arise when subsidiaries become more integrated with the MNE, and thus tend to be less responsive to domestic stimuli, market opportunities, etc. Trading groups and specialized staff groups are often established for the co-ordinating activities if a significant area office is not already in operation. The reduced responsiveness to local markets is due to the difficulty some MNEs have of being both integrated and locally responsive (differentiated) at the same time, without the high costs of a matrix organization.

Notes

1. For a discussion of implementation and staff specialists' role in providing external data on political instability see Kobrin (1982; pp. 87–110) and Keegan (1974) for a general review of environmental scanning.

2. For further description of the various kinds of MNE organizational structures discussed here see Stopford and Wells (1972), pp. 11–27.

3. For a very clear and practical description of the matrix structure see Stanley M. Davis and Paul R. Lawrence, *Matrix* (Addison-Wesley, 1977).

10 SUMMARY AND CONCLUSIONS

Government enforced intervention into the operation of MNE subsidiaries is usually costly to the MNE. Typically the response of MNEs has been to reduce overseas investments and to raise their profit requirements. Neither of these responses are satisfactory to the international firm nor most host nations.

The purpose of this book was to provide managers, consultants and students of MNEs with the information necessary to devise a better intervention management strategy. This strategy would describe how a firm could determine its bargaining position, monitor any changes and improve its position when necessary. This strategy was derived by examining patterns of intervention behaviour and patterns of business-government involvement across nations and industries. The successes and failures of firms which have implemented intervention management strategies were used to derive other lessons for successful implementation and integration.

Summary

This book is concerned with intervention risk. This is the probability of the host government enforcing policies which will force changes in the operations and strategies of the MNE. For reasons of clarity and accuracy, the oft-used term 'political risk' is used to define the risk that changes will take place in the political process through which intervention decisions are made. This would follow a coup or an electoral defeat. Thus defined, political risk applies to a nation, while intervention risk is firm-specific.

This subject is of interest because the traditional responses of MNEs to intervention are no longer effective. It appears to be almost impossible to select a 'safe' site for investment, almost all countries intervene. The safe, profitable Brazil of the 1960s and early 1970s turned into the costly interventionist Brazil of the 1980s.

Effects of Intervention

Intervention occurs because host-country nationals obtain financial and political benefits as a direct result. They become shareholders, distributors, component suppliers, or they take over part or all of the subsidiary's operation. Increased local sourcing and exports increase employment, while controls on financial transactions improve the fiscal picture. Any costs that occur from intervention are, unlike the benefits, long term in nature. This temporal gap between the long-term costs and the short-term benefits of intervention often results in excessive levels of intervention.

Although the effects on the MNE are well known one tends to forget how long term some of the costs are. Seemingly low-cost intervention like forced local sourcing, joint ventures, etc. raises cost and places the MNE at a strategic disadvantage. The firm is more vulnerable to competition — both domestic and other foreign — and becomes more dependent on the host government for financial support. The joint venture partner ideally suited to the MNE's early need for local skills and know-how, can become your competitor in the long term.

Basis of Intervention

Firms do not experience the same level of intervention because the host government discriminates. This discrimination, if it does not occur explicitly in the intervention policy, occurs during the enforcement phase.

The basis of this discrimination can be found in the different strategies and characteristics of subsidiaries. Such characteristics were thought not to play a role in intervention due to the high emotion or irrationality that usually existed. Today it is felt that most intervention decisions are rarely made arbitrarily or in an irrational manner. Even the most autocratic and revolutionary of governments appear to be aware of the economic realities. These realities suggest that governments intervene in subsidiaries whose characteristics suggest the benefits of intervention outweight the costs.

Determinants of Intervention

Those key characteristics which appear to determine the costs and benefits of intervention together define the bargaining power of the subsidiary. Those subsidiaries which experience intervention generally have less bargaining power than the host nation.

The allocation of bargaining power is determined by which party has control over, or access to, factors which are perceived to influence the continued success of the subsidiary in question. The MNE and the host nation compete in the supply of product and process technology, and managerial skills, with the MNE usually — but never always —

dominating. MNEs usually have complete control over the intra-MNE sourcing and exports, while the host controls access to its home market.

Other, non-bargaining power characteristics, also play a role. Subsidiary size and strategic importance feature, as do bilateral and multilateral agreements. Often mentioned but relatively unimportant in practice is industry type, political ideology and political stability.

Corporate Behaviour

In any system of relationships not only do differences in power influence the nature of the relationship, but so does the behaviour of the parties involved. Subsidiary executives can choose between a low-profile, uninvolved approach, and an activist one calling for frequent and direct contact with influential host nationals. The latter alternative is expensive, requiring executives experienced or trained in such activity. But it does allow subsidiary executives to influence domestic perceptions of the subsidiary and to learn more of intervention policies.

There appears to be a relationship between such corporate behaviour and intervention. While small subsidiaries can reasonably have a low-profile strategy without negative consequences, medium and large firms cannot. These larger firms are automatically involved in domestic affairs and hence will benefit from learning how to behave and from interacting with possible interventionists. In addition to ensuring that the MNE's bargaining position is transmitted to these interventionists, executives can collect useful intelligence about intervention sponsors, their goals and the real intent of intervention policies.

Managing Intervention: the Subsidiary

Based on the foregoing and on the successes and failures of several MNEs, a practical administrative procedure has been outlined for the successful management of intervention at the level of the subsidiary. This management system is based on modifying those corporate characteristics which determine the MNE's bargaining power.

Three steps, described in detail, are involved:

1. calculating the subsidiary's net bargaining power;
2. determining when and how to upgrade; and
3. how to implement the upgrade.

Different types of MNEs find particular kinds of bargaining power upgrades more feasible and easier to implement. MNEs with a limited product-line utilize new manufacturing processes; multi-product MNE, new products; vertically-integrated ones concentrate on intra-MNE sourcing, a rather effective source of bargaining power. Joint ventures, hampered as they are by the presence of local partners, have to rely on sourcing and exports more than any other due to the high dissipation rate of other upgrades. Strategically important subsidiaries have to take a completely different stand and increase the costs of intervention through the broad involvement of different firms and nations in its operation.

Nations, like firms, offer different opportunities for managing intervention. Host nations are at different levels of bargaining power and progress at different rates. There is also a strong suggestion that nations progress on different dimensions: some becoming far more adept at managerial than technical matters. Each situation requires a different management solution.

Managing Intervention: the Parent

The complexity of managing intervention at the global or regional level is the weakest link in this strategy. Factors MNEs must consider include the location of the intervention manager in the MNE's organizational structure, and the kind of executive − line or staff − to use for this activity. The management process has four stages:

1. data collection;
2. analysis and decision on intervention management activities;
3. implementation; and
4. integration.

The ten-year implementation timetable for a major MNE was provided as an illustration of this process.

Problems Remaining

The problem facing the incorporation of an intervention management strategy into a MNE are of two, independent, types. The first type of problem concerns the healthy hesitancy of MNEs to change dramatically their traditional approach to managing intervention. The second concerns problems of successfully implementing the strategy.

The intervention strategy proposed here runs contrary to the MNE's traditional response, and to the present response of international bankers to a similar situation. In response to the historically unpredictable nature of government intervention, most international firms and banks responded by reducing their asset exposure and increasing investment hurdle rates in the nation affected. The strategic shift required by this new management strategy brings with it the usual executive behaviours against change. Executives tend to concentrate on the more easily identified costs of managing intervention, for example, decreased margins because of forced exporting; higher capital and training requirements; etc. On the other hand, the benefits are not as identifiable and are longer term. Similar reactions to other strategic shifts in large firms, for example, computerization, the decision to invest overseas, an acquisition, suggest that time and leadership by senior management are the means of reducing the slow acceptance of the new strategy.

Successful implementation of this strategy requires executives who are prepared to spend several years in subsidiaries accumulating a significant amount of host-country knowledge. The level of technical and management skills must be higher, and frequently area offices need to be strengthened.

The 'problem' is that this can be very expensive in those MNEs used to sending executives abroad for three-year stints to manage subsidiaries producing mature products. The solution goes deep within the MNE, affecting reporting procedures, promotion policies, hiring practices and issues of technology transfer and training.

A related problem concerns the new executive activities successful intervention management requires. The most difficult one is the increased level of integration required because of inter-subsidiary sourcing, exporting and rapid new product and process introductions. While obtaining increased integration per se has its own difficulties, firms find that even more difficult are the costs from the reduced subsidiary autonomy and flexibility that often — but not necessarily — follows. A MNE with a centralized fully integrated organizational structure will find it difficult to respond to domestic opportunities, threats, preferences and political issues. Even for MNEs selling global products such a centralized structure has its costs.

Conclusion

This book is in response to attempts by multinational enterprises to deal with costly government intervention. The management strategy discussed is based on the fact that present day intervention is neither unpredictable nor unexplainable. That is not to say there are no unpredictable elements or chance, but those elements no longer dominate the discussion.

Intervention behaviour against foreign-owned firms appears to follow a similar pattern whether in Canada, Brazil or Tanzania. Governments discriminate among firms when making the decision to intervene. The basis of this discrimination can be traced to particular characteristics of the subsidiaries affected. Characteristics which collectively define the MNE's bargaining power determine the level of intervention. Because MNEs can change the strategy and character of their subsidiaries they can thereby affect their level of bargaining power. Because of the link between bargaining power and intervention we can now speak of managing intervention.

This management strategy is not easily implemented by all MNEs, not least of all because the costs of such a strategy are immediate while the benefits are longer term. However, several MNEs have been successful at implementation, and their experiences form a useful basis for a general strategy of intervention management.

Most MNEs are under considerable competitive pressure to manage globally with greater integration of subsidiary strategies, products, personnel and finances (Levitt, 1983). Intervention management also benefits greatly from such a global approach. The monitoring of bargaining power shifts, and the successful and profitable implementation of an intervention strategy is more easily accomplished in an integrated or globally-run MNE than in an MNE operated in a 'nation-based' fashion with relatively independent subsidiaries.

The successful management of intervention for an international firm is the successful management of the relationship between firm and sovereign government. Host governments, no matter how small, have the power and the right to intervene in the affairs of foreign-owned firms. Intervention management by MNEs implies an acceptance of this sovereign right as it allows firms to organize their affairs so as to accommodate such government action. MNEs will move on to other products and technologies as nations progress, and increase their economic contribution through more sourcing, exports and the like.

The benefits from the successful management of intervention are not one-sided. Successful management allows MNEs to continue foreign investment using subsidiaries with the longer-term horizons and the high flow of resources appropriate to conditions of relative stability and confidence. Host nations unambiguously benefit from this kind of MNE investment. So can MNEs.

BIBLIOGRAPHY

Andrews, Kenneth R. *The Concept of Corporate Strategy* (Irwin, Illinois, 1980)

Armstrong, A.B. 'Towards a Systems Approach to Foreign Wealth Deprivation in the Developing Countries' (unpublished PhD dissertation, University of Washington, 1972)

Beamish, Paul W. 'Joint Venture Performance in Developing Countries' (unpublished PhD dissertation, School of Business Administration, The University of Western Ontario, London, Canada, 1984)

Behrman, Jack N., J.J. Boddewyn, and Ashok Kapoor, *International Business Government Communications: U.S. Structures, Actors and Issues* (Lexington Books, Lexington, MA, 1975)

Berenbeim, Ronald E. *Operating Foreign Subsidiaries: How Independent Should They Be?* (Conference Board, New York, 1983)

Bradley, David G. 'Managing Against Expropriation', *Harvard Business Review* (July–August 1977), pp. 82 *eq seq.*

Business Week (26 July 1976) p. 50

Business Week, 'Tough Choices in Brazil: As the Junta Squeezes High-Tech Multinationals' (19 December 1983), p. 44

Crookell, Harold 'The Future of the US Direct Investment in Canada', *Business Quarterly* (Summer 1983)

Davis, Stanley M. 'Unity of Command versus Balance of Power: Two Models of Management', *Sloan Management Review* (1975)

Davis, Stanley M. and Michael Beer, 'Creating a Global Organization: Failures Along the Way', *Columbia Journal of World Business* (Summer 1976)

Fagre, Nathan and Louis T. Wells Jr, 'The Bargaining Power of Multinationals and Host Government', *Journal of International Business Studies* (Fall 1982)

Franko, L.G. *Joint Venture Survival in Multinational Corporations* (Praeger, New York, 1971)

Galbraith, Jay R. and Daniel A. Nathanson, *Strategy Implementation: The Role of Structure and Process* (West Publishing, St Paul, 1978)

Gasser, Thomas P. and Rossier, Jacques A. 'Lessons from Switzerland's Mini-Multinationals', *The McKinsey Quarterly* (Winter 1974), pp. 32 *et seq.*

Haendel, Dan H., Gerald T. West, and Robert G. Meadow, *Overseas Investment and Political Risk* (Foreign Policy Research Institute, Philadelphia, 1975)

Hawkins, Robert G., Norman Mintz, and Provissiero 'Government Takeovers of US Foreign Affiliates', *Journal of International Business Studies* (Spring 1976), pp. 3–16

Hirschman, Albert O. *Development Projects Observed* (Brookings Institute, Washington, 1967)

Keegan, Warren S. 'Multinational Scanning: A Study of the Information Sources Utilized by Headquarters Executives in Multinational Companies', *Administrative Science Quarterly*, no. 19 (1974), pp. 411–21

Killing, J.P. 'Making Global Joint Ventures Work', *Harvard Business Review*

(May/June 1982)

—— *Strategies for Joint Venture Success* (Croom Helm, London; Praeger, New York, 1983)

Kobrin, Stephen J. 'The Environmental Determinants of Foreign Direct Manufacturing Investment: An Ex-Post Empirical Analysis', *Journal of International Business Studies* (Fall-Winter 1976), pp. 29-41

—— 'Political Risk: A Review and Reconsideration', *Journal of International Business Studies* (Spring-Summer 1979)

—— 'Foreign Enterprise and Forced Divestment in LDCs', *International Organization*, no. 34 (1980), pp. 65-88

—— *Managing Political Risk Assessment* (University of California Press, 1982)

Lecraw, Donald J. 'Bargaining Power, Ownership and Profitability of Subsidiaries of Transnational Corporations in Developing Countries', *Journal of International Business Studies* (Spring-Summer 1984)

Levitt, Theodore 'The Globalization of Markets', *Harvard Business Review* (May-June 1983), pp. 92-102

March, James G. and Herbert A. Simon, *Organizations* (John Wiley & Sons, New York, 1958)

Moran, Theodore H. *Multinational Corporations and the Politics of Dependence: Copper in Chile* (Princeton University Press 1974)

—— 'The International Political Economy of Cuban Nickel Development' in Cole Blasier and Carmelo Mesa-Cargo (eds), *Cuba in the World* (University of Pittsburg Press, Pittsburg, Pennsylvania, 1979)

—— (ed.) *International Political Risk Assessment: The State of the Art* (Georgetown University School of Foreign Service, Washington, DC, 1980)

Moran, Theodore H. and Debbie Havens Maddox, *Transnational Corporations in the Copper Industry* (UN Centre on Transnational Corporations, New York, 1981)

Parvin, Manoucher 'Economic Determinants of Political Unrest', *Journal of Conflict Revolution*, no. 17 (1973), pp. 271-95

Perlmutter, Howard V. 'Attitudinal Patterns in Joint Decision-Making in Multinational Firms – Nation State Relationships', in Mathew Tuite, Richard Chisholm and Michael Radnor, *Interorganizational Decision-Making* (Aldine Publishing Company, Chicago, 1972), pp. 201-21

Poynter, Thomas A. 'Multinational Enterprises and Political Risk in Less-Developed Countries: An Analysis of the Corporate Determinants of Host Country Intervention' (PhD dissertation, London Graduate School of Business Studies, London, 1978)

—— 'Government Intervention in Less-Developed Countries: The Experience of Multinational Companies', *Journal of International Business Studies* (Spring-Summer 1982), pp. 9-25

Poynter, Thomas A. and Allan M. Rugman, 'World Product Mandates: How Will Multinationals Respond?', *Business Quarterly* (October 1982)

Poynter, Thomas A. and Roderick E. White, 'Strategies for Foreign Owned Firms in Canada', *Business Quarterly* (Summer 1984)

Prahalad, C.K. and Yves L. Doz, 'An Approach to Strategic Control in MNC's and 'Headquarters Influence and Strategic Control in MNCs', *Sloan Management Review* (Summer 1981, Fall 1981)

Robock, Stefan 'Political Risk: Identification and Assessment', *Columbia Journal of World Business* (July-August 1971), pp. 6–20

Root, Franklin 'Analyzing Political Risks in International Business', in A. Kapoor and Philip D. Grub (eds) *The Multinational Enterprise in Transition* (Darwin Press, Princeton, 1972)

—— 'The Management by LDC Governments of the Political Risk Trade-Off in Direct Foreign Investment' (paper presented to the International Studies Association, Toronto, 1976)

Schaan, J.L. 'Parent Control and Joint Venture Success: The Case of Mexico' (unpublished PhD dissertation, School of Business Administration, The University of Western Ontario, London, Canada, 1983)

Stopford, John M. and Louis T. Wells, Jr, *Managing the Multinational Enterprise: Organization of the Firm and Ownership of the Subsidiaries* (Basic Books, Inc., New York, 1972)

Truitt, J.F. 'Expropriation of Private Foreign Investment: A Framework to Consider the Post World War II Experience of British and American Investors' (PhD dissertation, Indiana University, 1970) pp. 194–6

United Nations, 'Transnational Corporations in World Development: Third Survey' (United Nations Centre on Transnational Corporation, 1983), pp. 55–104

Vernon, Raymond 'Foreign-Owned Enterprise and the Developing Countries', *Public Policy* (1966), p. 36

—— *Sovereignty at Bay: The Multinational Spread of U.S. Enterprises* (Basic Books, Inc., New York, 1971), pp. 26–59

Wall Street Journal, 'Overseas Work' (19 July 1983), p. 1

INDEX

.